SCHOOL NEEDLEWORK

*A Course of Study in Sewing designed
for use in Schools*

BY

OLIVE C. HAPGOOD
Teacher of Sewing in Boston Public Schools

" Learn the sound qualities of all useful stuffs, and make everything of the best you can get, whatever its price. . . . and then, every day, make some little piece of useful clothing, sewn with your own fingers as strongly as it can be stitched; and embroider it or otherwise beautify it moderately with fine needlework, such as a girl may be proud of having done."
— John Ruskin.

TEACHER'S EDITION

BOSTON, U.S.A.
GINN & COMPANY, PUBLISHERS
1893

COPYRIGHT, 1893,
BY OLIVE C. HAPGOOD

ALL RIGHTS RESERVED.

Ginn & Company
The Athenæum Press
Boston

Printing Statement:

Due to the very old age and scarcity of this book, many of the pages may be hard to read due to the blurring of the original text, possible missing pages, missing text, dark backgrounds and other issues beyond our control.

Because this is such an important and rare work, we believe it is best to reproduce this book regardless of its original condition.

Thank you for your understanding.

PREFACE.

The importance of instruction in sewing in the Public School is now generally recognized. As manual training comes into greater prominence, new methods and helps are necessary. The demand for these was felt by the author, and this book is the result of practical experience in the class-room. Its purpose is to assist both teacher and pupil; lightening the teacher's labors by saving constant repetition, and giving the pupil a manual for reference, with the hope that the information thus acquired will assist in fitting her for the duties of life. Simplicity with completeness has been the aim throughout.

In the teacher's edition, the work is further supplemented by practical hints and suggestions as to successful methods of teaching the lessons, and by courses of study for Kindergarten, Primary, and Industrial Sewing. It also contains a list of articles obtainable for a sewing cabinet, and talks on kindred subjects.

The author wishes to acknowledge her indebtedness to the teachers who have so kindly assisted her, and to members of the School Board for their advice and interest in the preparation of the work.

CONTENTS.

PART I.
	PAGE
GENERAL DIRECTIONS	1

PART II.
PLAIN SEWING	13

PART III.
ORNAMENTAL STITCHES	115

PART IV.
DRAFTING, CUTTING AND MAKING GARMENTS	129

TEACHER'S SUPPLEMENT.
TEACHING THE LESSONS	163
COURSE OF SEWING	172
PRACTICAL SUGGESTIONS	176
KINDERGARTEN SEWING	187
PRIMARY SEWING	199
COURSE OF SEWING FOR INDUSTRIAL SCHOOLS	220
FACTS FOR OBSERVATION LESSONS	222
SCHOOL-CABINET	239
INDEX	243

PART I.

GENERAL DIRECTIONS.

Dear Girls: You have now become old enough to prepare for woman's duties; one of these is the art of sewing, which we will take up as simply as possible. By following the given directions carefully, you will become able to dress your dolls, assist your mothers in mending, make garments, fancy articles, etc.

A convenient outfit for your school sewing consists of a bag large enough to hold certain necessary materials and the garment to be made. The bag should be made of dark or medium-colored cloth, so that it may not soil easily, and should have a strong gathering tape.

The following articles are needed. — 1. Half a yard of bleached or half-bleached cotton cloth for a trial-piece and sample work.

2. Spools of white cotton, Nos. 40–80, also one of No. 50 colored cotton for basting.

3. A well-fitting silver or celluloid thimble, for the second finger of the right hand.

4. An emery bag to brighten the needle, when it does not go through the cloth easily.

5. A paper of Nos. 5–10 ground-down needles.

6. A pinball well filled with small pins.

7. A tape measure.

8. A piece of wax.

9. A pair of scissors, for girls in the higher classes.

Your name should be written with ink on the bag, paper of needles, spools of thread, and sample cloth. An easy way to remember the necessary articles is to let the hand represent the cloth ; the thumb, the bag ; the first finger, the spools of cotton ; the second finger, the thimble and emery bag ; the third finger, the needles and pins ; and the fourth finger, the tape measure and wax.

Directions for putting away the work. — 1. Before folding the work, run the needle in and out of the cloth, near the last stitches, so as to keep it secure and aid in finding the place at the next sewing lesson.

2. To fold the work, smooth it out, fold it lengthwise and narrow enough to go into the bag ; then fold it the opposite way.

3. Put the thimble into the bag first, as it is apt to be forgotten.

4. After all the articles are placed in the bag, draw it up closely.

5. Wind the tape tightly around the bag until about six inches of it are left.

6. Place two fingers of the left hand over the coil of tape, and wind once over the fingers and around the bag.

7. As the fingers are withdrawn, slip the end of the tape through, and draw tightly.

If the above directions are carefully observed, no girl should report any missing article at the next lesson.

Directions for sewing. — 1. Be very careful to have clean hands.

2. Sit in an erect position, never resting any part of the arm on the desk.

3. Do not fasten the work to the desk or knee.

4. Never sew without a thimble, either the top or the side of it can be used.

5. Do not put the work or thread to the mouth, as that will soil it.

6. In plain sewing, begin to sew at the end of the cloth, or at a seam, *holding the part of the work not sewed in the left hand.*

7. When scissors are not used, to break the thread place the left thumb-nail firmly over the last stitches; wind the thread around the right forefinger, and break the thread with the right thumb-nail.

8. Do all sewing nicely, making the stitches small and even, having the wrong side look as neat as possible, and sewing the corners with great care.

9. When obliged to take out the stitches, use the eye of a needle, and pick out one stitch at a time; in stitching, pick out the thread on one side, then on the other.

10. Before showing the work to the teacher, fasten the needle securely in the work.

We will call the fleshy or soft part of the forefinger a sewing cushion.

What are the necessary articles for school sewing? Upon which finger is the thimble worn? For what is an emery bag used? Where should the needle be placed before putting away the work? What should first be put into the bag? Why should the bag be tied up carefully? In what condition should the hands be? How should a child sit while sewing? Should the work be fastened to the desk or knee? Should you ever sew without a thimble? Should the work or thread be put to the mouth? Why? In plain sewing where should you begin to sew? In which hand should the part of the work not sewed be held? How should the thread be broken? How ought all sewing to be done? Where should great care be taken? What is called the sewing cushion?

NEEDLES AND THREAD.

Needles. — A needle is a small piece of steel, pointed at one end, and having an eye at the other to receive a thread.

Needles are of various sizes and shapes, according to the uses for which they are intended.

Three kinds of needles are used in sewing on cotton cloth, — sharps, ground-downs, and betweens ; the sizes range from No. 1, the largest, to No. 12, the smallest. Sharps are long needles, ground-downs are shorter, and betweens are still shorter. Ground-downs are excellent for school use, as they do not bend or break easily. Betweens are used for heavy work.

Worsted and darning needles are used for yarn, and are of different sizes. Worsted needles have a long eye, and either a sharp or a blunt point. A very long needle is used in millinery work. A bodkin or tape needle has a long eye, and is used for running tape into a hem or casing.

Let us examine our paper of needles. It is assorted so that we may have needles suitable for all kinds of stitches. To open it, place a finger between the folds of the paper and separate them. Now, opening the sides and short ends which cover the needles, we find twenty-five needles in a secure case. Keep them in their places so that we may know the proper size to use for the thread or stitch. Beginning at the middle, we find three No. 5 needles, which should be used only with very coarse thread ; they are suitable for sewing on boot-buttons, etc. The needles on each side are alike, so following down one

NEEDLES AND THREAD.

side, we find two No. 6 needles, used for sewing on coarse materials ; next are three No. 7 needles, suitable for hemming on towels, etc. ; then there are three No. 8 needles, for stitching ; next are two No. 9 needles, used in hemming cotton cloth ; and the last is a No. 10 needle, for very fine work.

After taking out a needle, fold and tie up the paper so that none may drop out. Never use a bent needle, as it makes uneven stitches. In passing a needle, hand the eye of the needle to the person, keeping the point towards yourself.

Thread. — A small twist made from flax, silk, cotton, or wool, is called thread. Thread made from flax is called linen thread, and is very strong. Thread made from silk is called silk or twist, and is used when sewing on nice textures. Cotton thread can be obtained in many numbers, and is used when sewing on wash goods ; the finer the thread, the higher the number. Thread made from wool is called yarn, worsted, zephyr, etc., and is used for darning, canvas-work, and fancy-work.

A new spool of thread can be unfastened by slipping a pin under the thread, where it is caught in the wood. To unwind the thread, hold the spool in the left hand, with the end of the thread between two fingers. Unwind the thread until it is of the required length. Break it by holding it securely in each hand, and snapping it across the ends of the thumbs. When not using a spool of thread, keep the end of the thread fastened in the wood.

Use a piece of thread the length of the desk, or about as long as the arm. When using very fine thread, take a shorter needleful. If the thread kinks, remove the needle, and beginning at the work, draw the thread tightly between the thumb-nail and the end of the forefinger. To prevent thread from kinking, thread the needle with the end that hangs from the spool. When using double thread, as in gathering, sewing on buttons, etc., before making the knot, draw the double thread, beginning at the needle, across the wax.

Threading the needle. — 1. Sit erect, bringing the needle and thread as close to the eyes as necessary.

2. Roll the end of the thread between the thumb and cushion of the forefinger, so as to twist it tightly.

3. Hold the needle steadily between the thumb and forefinger of the left hand, with the eye a little above.

4. Take the end of the thread between the thumb and forefinger of the right hand, letting about half-an-inch protrude, and put the thread through the eye of the needle.

If preferred, the thread can be held in the left hand, and the eye of the needle passed over it.

To aid in threading a round-eyed needle with worsted or loosely twisted thread, a few fibres of cotton-batting or a fine thread can be rolled over the end. Waxing the end of the thread before rolling it, is also helpful.

Threading a long-eyed needle. — 1. Hold the end of the zephyr between the left thumb and forefinger, allowing half-an-inch to show.

2. Place the pointed end of the needle on the cushion of the forefinger, and over the zephyr.

3. With the left thumb fold the end of the zephyr tightly over the needle.

4. Withdraw the needle, and pass the eye of the needle over the loop of zephyr.

Knots. — To make a knot, as in Fig. 1, wind the thread around two or three fingers, and crossing it, put the end through the loop.

To bring a knot close to the end of the thread. — 1. With the thumb and forefinger of the right hand, take hold of the thread a few inches from the end.

Fig. 1. — Showing the thread in a knot before it is drawn up.

2. Wind the end around the forefinger of the left hand, about midway of the finger-nail.

3. Pressing tightly, roll the end of the thread downward on the side of the thumb, twisting it once or twice.

4. Bring the second finger upon the thumb, and over the thread.

5. Lifting the forefinger, draw up the thread with the right hand.

The knot can also be made with the right hand.

To fasten the thread in sewing, take two or three stitches in the same place, or sew back a few stitches. Fasten silk very securely as it is apt to work out.

When learning to sew, it is best to use *colored thread* on white cloth, as it makes the stitches plainer, and mistakes are more easily seen. For colored work, choose thread or silk a shade darker than the material, as it will work lighter. Twist is twirled the opposite way from cotton thread.

The size of the needle and thread to be used, depends upon the quality of the work. A coarse needle and thread are used for coarse work, and a fine needle and thread for fine work.

The numbers of needles and thread needed for the different kinds of stitches in cotton cloth:—

Hemming,
Tucking, } No. 9 needle, No. 70 or 80 thread.

Running,
Stitching,
Overhanding,
Overcasting, } No. 8 needle, No. 50 or 60 thread.

Button-holes, No. 7 or 8 needle, No. 40 or 50 thread.

Basting,
Gathering, } No. 7 or 8 needle, No. 36 or 40 thread.

What is a needle? Why is an assorted paper of needles necessary? Why should they be kept in their places in the paper? Why should the paper of needles be kept tied up? How should a needle be passed to any one? What is thread? What is thread made from flax called? What is thread made from silk called? What is said about cotton thread? What is thread made from wool called? How is thread broken from the spool? How long a piece of thread should be used? If it kinks what should be done? Which end of the thread should be put into the needle? What is done to the end of the thread before threading the needle? What part of the finger should the thread be wound around, in order to bring a knot close to the end of the thread? How many times should the thread be twisted, when rolling it down the side of the thumb? What is the next thing to do? Next? How is thread fastened in sewing? When should a coarse needle and thread be used? A fine needle and thread? What size needle and thread should be used on cotton cloth for hemming? tucking? running? stitching? overhanding? overcasting? button-holes? basting? gathering?

CLOTH.

Cloth is a fabric woven from cotton, wool, linen, or silk. Cotton is the cheapest, and silk the most expensive in price. From cotton are made many qualities of unbleached, half-bleached, and bleached cloth, also calicoes, ginghams, muslins, nainsooks, cambrics, etc. From wool are made flannels, cashmeres, and many varieties of dress goods. Linen cloth is made in all grades, from the finest linen lawn to heavy canvas; it is generally used for collars, cuffs, handkerchiefs, table-cloths, napkins, towels, etc. Silk is made into dress-silks, ribbons, satins, velvets, etc. Soft, pliable, white cotton cloth (often called muslin) of medium quality is best for a beginner to use at first.

The threads of the cloth are called the warp and the woof. The threads running lengthwise are the *warp*, those running across from selvedge to selvedge are the *woof;* both can be easily seen on a piece of coarse crash. The warp is usually stronger than the woof, and for this reason, any part of a garment requiring strength, should be cut lengthwise of the cloth.

Cloth is woven straight, but is sometimes drawn out of shape by pressing. When you can ravel a thread the width or length of the cloth, it is straight, or will become so after washing. If it looks uneven, it can be drawn into place by stretching it on the bias. Calico, when torn, often looks very uneven, and should be pulled into shape.

The *selvedge* of cloth is the finished lengthwise edge, and cannot be ravelled. The *raw edge* is the edge that is cut or torn. A *fold* is the edge made by doubling one part of the cloth over the other. The *nap* is the shaggy substance on the surface of the cloth. *To tear* a piece of cloth, cut in one inch by a thread, then, holding a corner of the cut between the thumb and forefinger of each hand, roll the edges from you, and tear steadily; a fine piece of cloth must be torn carefully.

What is cloth? Name some kinds of cloth made from cotton; from wool; from linen; from silk. What are the threads of the cloth running lengthwise of the goods called? Those running across? How can you tell when a piece of cotton cloth is straight? If it looks uneven, how can it be drawn into shape? What is the selvedge of cloth? The raw edge? What is a fold? How should a piece of cloth be torn?

SCISSORS AND CUTTING.

A pair of scissors is an instrument used for cutting, consisting of two blades crossing each other, and moving on a pivot.

Scissors are of many sizes. Large scissors are called shears (Fig. 2, *c*), and small scissors with the ends of the blades rounded are called pocket scissors (Fig. 2, *d*), as they are convenient to carry in the pocket. In shears, the round bow is for the thumb, and the oval bow is for two of the fingers; one blade is more pointed than the other, and when cutting this blade should be held down-

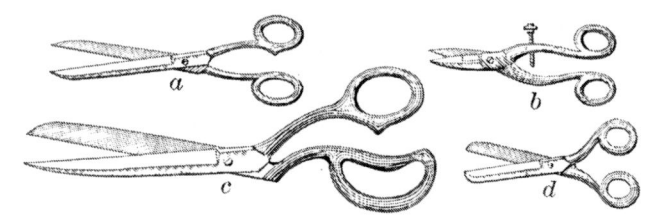

Fig. 2.—*a*, Showing ladies' scissors; *b*, button-hole scissors; *c*, shears; *d*, pocket scissors.

ward. In button-hole scissors (Fig. 2, *b*) a screw is attached to regulate the size of the button-hole. When passing scissors, hand the bows to the person, keeping the point towards yourself.

In order to cut straight, draw out a thread of the cloth, and cut along the line thus made (for drawing a thread, see page 116). In materials from which a thread cannot be easily drawn, fold the cloth where it is to be cut, pin the selvedges together on each side, crease, and cut on the crease. In materials in which the threads are plainly marked, either by plaids or stripes, there is no need of drawing a thread or folding the cloth.

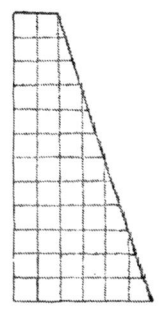

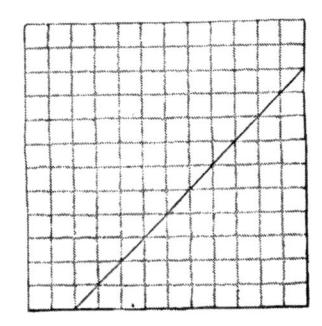

Fig. 3. — Showing a bias cut.   Fig. 4. — Showing an exact bias cut.

To cut bias, cut on a slanting line across both the warp and the woof.

To cut an exact bias, lay the selvedge or a warp thread of the cloth, on a line with a woof thread, and cut on the fold.

<small>What is a pair of scissors? Name the different kinds of scissors. How should shears be held? How can cloth be cut straight? How can it be cut when a thread is not easily drawn? How is an exact bias cut?</small>

PART II.

PLAIN SEWING.

Sewing is work done with the needle and thread.

The following directions should be before the pupil during class work.[1]

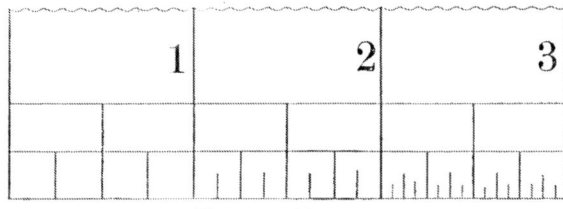

Fig. 5. — Measure.

The above represents a three inch rule, to use when certain measurements are required. The first inch is divided into halves and quarters, the second inch into eighths, and the third inch into sixteenths.

Fractions of a yard: —

        3 feet or 36 inches is a yard.
        27 inches is three quarters of a yard.
        18 inches is one half of a yard.
        9 inches is a quarter of a yard.
        4½ inches is an eighth of a yard.
        2¼ inches is a sixteenth of a yard.

* How many inches in a yard? Three quarters of a yard? One half? A quarter? An eighth? A sixteenth?

[1] The illustrations generally represent the stitches enlarged.

DRILLS.

Drill No. 1. — For practice in using the needle and thimble.

Materials. — A needle and a thimble.

Directions. — 1. Place the thimble on the second finger of the right hand.

2. Hold the pointed end of the needle between the end of the thumb and forefinger of the right hand.

3. Place the thimble on the eye of the needle.

4. Push the needle between the thumb and forefinger, being careful not to cramp the other fingers.

5. With the left hand push the point back into its former position.

6. Repeat until it can be done easily.

Drill No. 2. — For practice in the motion of stitching, hemming, etc.

Materials. — No. 8 needle, No. 50 thread, and a strip of white cotton cloth.

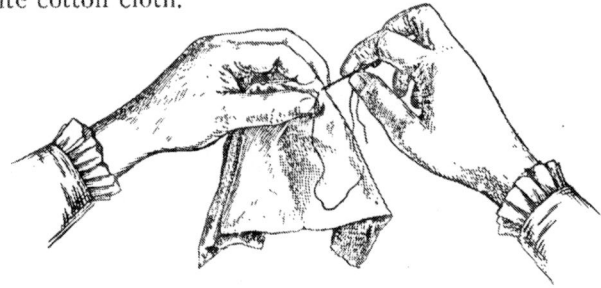

Fig. 6 — Showing the work and hands in position.

Directions. — 1. Thread the needle, but make no knot.

2. Hold the cloth over the forefinger of the left hand,

keeping it in place with the thumb and second finger, as in Fig. 6.

3. Hold the needle between the thumb and the forefinger of the right hand.

4. Insert the needle from right to left, taking up a little of the cloth, and push the needle nearly through.

5. Take the pointed end of the needle between the thumb and cushion of the forefinger of the right hand.

6. Draw the needle and thread through, bringing the thimble finger down near the forefinger, with the thread passing between the third and little fingers. Keep the little finger nearly straight to guide the thread.

7. Repeat until the motion is learned.

Drill No. 3. — For practice in the motion of basting, running, gathering, etc.

Materials. — No. 8 needle, No. 50 thread, and a strip of cotton cloth.

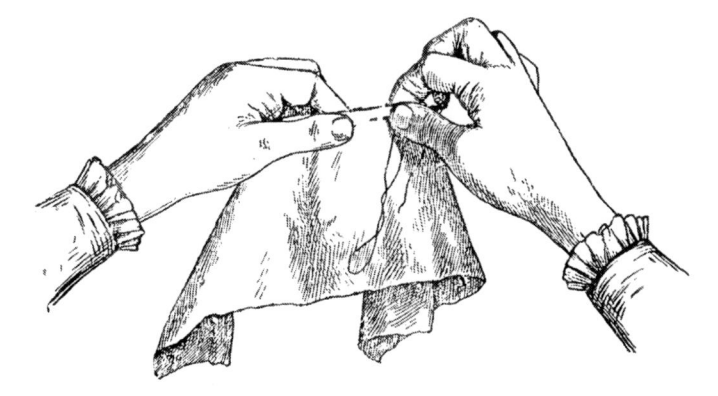

Fig. 7. — Showing the work and hands in position.

16 SCHOOL NEEDLEWORK.

Directions. — 1. Have the needle threaded, but make no knot.

2. Hold the cloth between the thumb and forefinger of each hand, as in Fig. 7.

3. With the right elbow away from the side, put the point of the needle through a few threads of the cloth, placing the thumb and forefinger of the right hand over it.

4. Pressing the end of the thimble against the eye of the needle, take three or more stitches in the cloth over the cushion of the left forefinger, moving only the elbow joint. (Fig. 7.)

5. Draw the needle and thread through as in Drill No. 2.

6. Repeat until the motion is learned.

Drill No. 4. — For practice in the motion of overcasting.

Materials. — No. 8 needle, No. 50 thread, and a folded edge of cotton cloth.

Fig. 8. — Showing the work and hand in position.

Directions. — 1. Have the needle threaded, but make no knot.

DRILLS.

2. Hold the fold of the cloth slanting across the edge of the cushion of the left forefinger, keeping it in place with the thumb and second finger, as in Fig. 8.

3. Put the needle in from the back of the fold, pointing it towards the left shoulder.

4. Draw the needle and thread through as in Drill No. 2.

Drill No. 5. — For practice in the motion of overhanding.

Materials. — No. 8 needle, No. 50 thread, and a folded edge of cotton cloth.

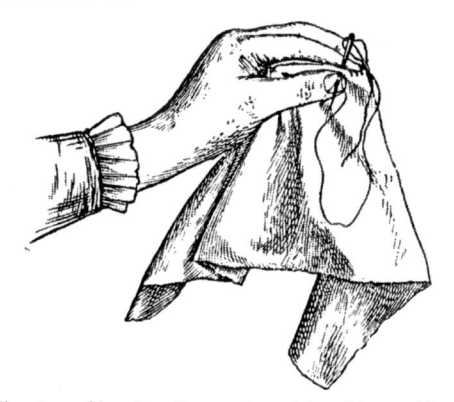

Fig. 9. — Showing the work and hand in position.

Directions. — 1. Have the needle threaded, but make no knot.

2. Hold the fold of cloth horizontally along the edge of the cushion of the left forefinger, and around the end of the finger, keeping it in place with the thumb and second finger, as in Fig. 9.

3. Hold the right elbow away from the side, without bending the wrist, and so that the palm of the hand is towards you.

4. Insert the needle from the back of the fold, pointing it directly towards the chest.

5. Draw the needle and thread through as in Drill No. 2.

CANVAS-WORK.

The stitches in sewing can be easily learnt on canvas, using bright-colored single or split zephyr, according to the quality of the canvas.

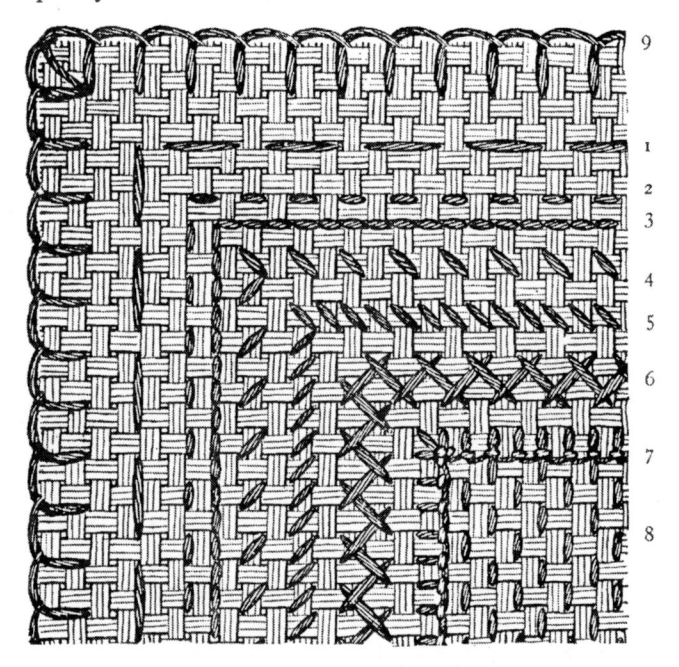

Fig. 10. — Showing different stitches taken on canvas.

CREASING AND PINCHING.

Fig. 10 represents a corner of a square of canvas, with the stitches taken in the following order: —

1. Uneven basting.
2. Running.
3. Stitching.
4. Overcasting.
5. Overhanding.
6. Catch-stitch.
7. Button-hole stitch.
8. Darning.
9. The edges are worked with the blanket or loop-stitch.

CREASING AND PINCHING.

A crease for sewing is made by folding the cloth, and pressing the edge until a line is made, which serves to sew on.

Materials. — A ten-inch strip of bleached or half-bleached cotton cloth. (A more distinct line can be made on the bleached than on the half-bleached cotton cloth.)

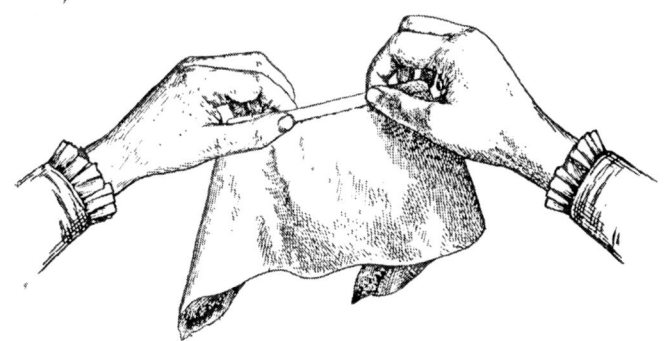

Fig. 11. — Showing the position of the hands.

Creasing. — 1. Hold the cloth firmly with the hands as in Fig. 11.

2. Beginning at the upper right-hand end of the cloth, turn down towards you the edge one-fourth of an inch in depth, for three or four inches.

3. Holding the cloth tightly between the hands, crease the edge with the end of the thumb-nail and the cushion of the left forefinger, until it will remain flat and has a sharp edge.

4. Fold and crease the next three inches in the same manner, and so continue to the end.

5. Holding the right-hand corner of the fold firmly, crease the entire length.

Pinching. — 1. At the right end of the crease, lay a half-inch fold between the thumb and forefinger of the right hand.

2. Lay another over this, and so on, until all the cloth is folded.

3. Pinch the folds, and turn up the edge.

4. Turn the other side of the cloth towards you, and the sharp edge will serve *as a line to sew on.*

If the cloth has been well creased, pinching is seldom necessary.

What is a crease? What purpose does it serve in sewing? How should you hold the cloth in creasing? At which end should you begin? How is the edge turned? How is it creased? How should the edge of the fold look? After the cloth has been once creased, what should be done to the entire length? After turning up the edge, what should be done? Why?

BASTING.

Basting is done by taking long stitches to keep the cloth in place for sewing.

Materials. — No. 8 needle, No. 50 colored thread, pins, and a half-yard strip of cotton cloth, with one of the long sides creased.

Fig. 12. — Showing even basting stitches, needle inserted.

In even basting, make the stitches short and alike on both sides. This method of basting is used for the seams of a dress-waist, or for several thicknesses of cloth.

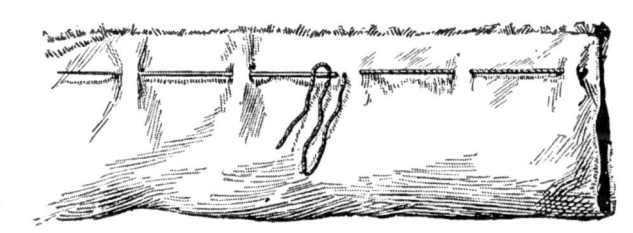

Fig. 13. — Showing uneven basting stitches, needle in position.

In uneven basting, take stitches half-an-inch long on the upper side, and as small as possible on the under side. This is the proper basting for ordinary work, as the stitches serve for a guide in sewing.

22   SCHOOL NEEDLEWORK.

The basting, in Fig. 14, is done by taking one long and two short stitches alternately.

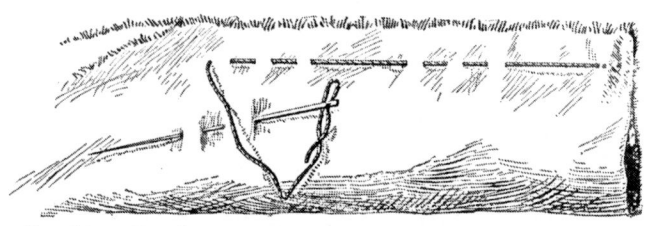

Fig. 14.— Showing a method of basting used on heavy cloth, needle in the proper position for putting away the work.

Basting. — Practise Drill No. 3 (page 15).
1. Make a knot in the thread to hold it securely.
2. Begin at the right-hand side of the cloth.
3. Place the right-hand corners exactly together, having the sharp edge of the crease towards you.

Fig. 15.— Showing the needle in position for beginning.

4. Insert the needle on the crease one-eighth of an inch from the end of the cloth, and take up a few threads (Fig. 15).
5. Let the needle remain in the cloth, and pin the opposite ends together, by placing a pin vertically through the cloth.
6. Put a pin in the middle vertically.

7. Draw the needle through, and proceed with the basting required, holding the work as in Fig. 7 (page 15), taking each stitch on the crease, and *keeping the edges even*.

8. Fasten the thread securely by taking three or four stitches in the same place.

Suggestions. — Never sew without basting, or when the threads are loose. If a child tries to sew without having the work basted, it will pucker, and must be ripped out. The short stitches on the under side keep the cloth in place, and prevent it from slipping. Take short basting stitches for hand work, but longer stitches may be taken for machine sewing. When learning to baste, only one stitch at a time should be taken, but later several stitches can be taken before drawing the needle through. Basting threads should be taken out when the work is finished.

<small>How is basting done? How are the stitches made in even basting? For what purpose is even basting used? How should uneven basting stitches be taken? What is the first step in basting? Where begin? What should be done to the corners? How must the edges be held? Where do you insert the needle? Before drawing it through, what should be done? Where should each stitch be taken? How should the thread be fastened? What purpose do the short stitches on the under side serve? When the work is finished, what should be done?</small>

STITCHING.

Stitching is done by taking a stitch backward on the upper side of the cloth, and a longer stitch forward on the under side, making the stitches meet.

Materials. — No. 8 needle, No. 50 thread, and a half yard strip of cotton cloth, doubled and basted.

Stitching. — Practise Drill No. 2 (page 14).

24   SCHOOL NEEDLEWORK.

1. Make a *small* knot in the thread.

2. Hold the work over the cushion of the left forefinger, as in Fig. 6 (page 14).

3. Insert the needle at the right-hand corner of the cloth, between the edges of the seam, one-eighth of an inch from the end, and one thread of the cloth below the basting.

4. Draw the needle and thread through.

5. Put the point of the needle back a few threads from where the needle comes through the cloth, and bring it out the same distance beyond.

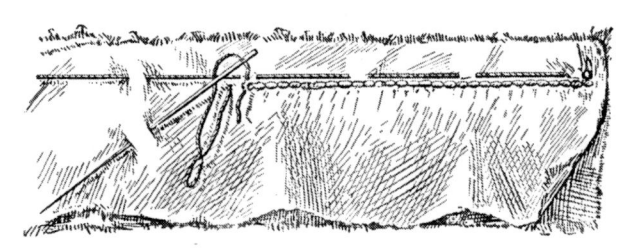

Fig. 16. — Showing the stitches

6. Continue, putting the needle back each time into the last stitch.

7. Make the stitches even and keep the seam straight (Fig. 16), leaving one thread of the cloth between the stitches and the basting.

8. Fasten the thread, by inverting the cloth, and taking a few stitches directly over the last ones made.

9. Join the thread, by making a small knot, and concealing it in the seam; or by taking one stitch with the new thread, leaving half-an-inch of the thread to be brought to the left, and to be sewed over with the next few stitches, allowing it to wind in and out.

Suggestions. — In the same manner sew all seams having raw edges, if a strain is coming on them, as in shoulder seams, the seams of drawers, etc. A bias seam should be sewed from the broad part to the narrow.

<small>How is stitching done? How is the work held? Where is the needle first inserted? Where next? Where is it brought out? As you continue, where should the needle always be inserted? How should the stitches be made? How many threads of the cloth should be left between the basting and the stitches? How should the thread be fastened? How should the thread be joined?</small>

HALF-BACKSTITCHING.

Fig. 17. — Showing the stitches and the needle in position.

Half-backstitching is the same as stitching, except that the needle is put only half-way back, thus leaving a space between the stitches (Fig. 17).

<small>How does half-backstitching differ from stitching?</small>

HEMMING.

A hem is a fold, made by twice turning over the edge of a piece of cloth, and then sewing it down.

Materials. — No. 9 needle, No. 70 thread, and a strip of cotton cloth.

To prepare the hem, make a fold one-fourth of an inch wide, and crease; then fold again one-fourth of an inch deep and crease. Baste near the edge of the first fold with uneven basting stitches. For wider hems, have the first fold one-fourth of an inch wide, being careful to crease it thoroughly, as much depends upon this; crease the second fold the required width, which can be done evenly, by measuring every two inches with a paper or other measure. If a very wide hem is required, baste as you measure, first along the upper edge of the hem, and then along the lower edge. On woollen cloth, baste down the first narrow fold, then baste as for a hem on cotton cloth.

Fig. 18. — Showing the needle in position for beginning the work.

Hemming. — Practise Drill No. 2 (page 14).

1. Have no knot in the thread.
2. Hold the hem across the cushion of the left forefinger, as in Fig. 6 (page 14).
3. Pointing the needle from you, insert it at the edge of the fold, one-third of an inch from the right-hand end, and bring it out close to the end, as in Fig. 18.
4. Carefully draw the needle through, leaving a little of the thread at the end, to be tucked under the hem with

HEMMING. 27

the point of the needle, and to be sewed down with the first stitches.

5. Take up one or two threads of the cloth, and one or two threads of the fold, keeping the needle on a line with the hem, and pointing towards the left shoulder.

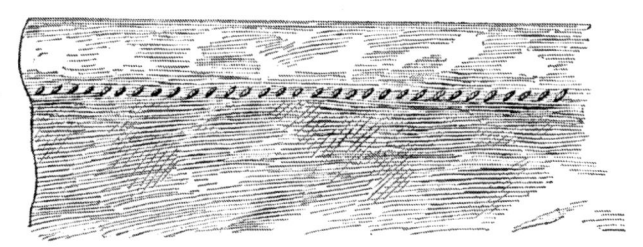

Fig. 19. — Showing the work as it looks on the right side.

6. Draw the needle out and continue, making the stitches close and slanting (Figs. 19 and 20).

7. When the thread becomes too short for use, either cut or break it.

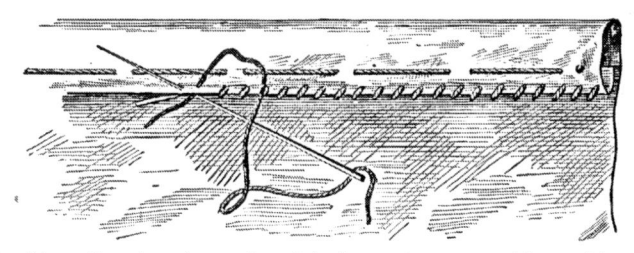

Fig. 20. — Showing the work as it looks on the wrong side; and how to join the thread, the double line representing the old thread, and the black line the new thread.

8. To join the thread (Fig. 20). If there is no end left of the thread, pick out a few stitches, always *leaving the end between the hem*. With the needle, draw the end under the fold, and towards the thumb. Begin with a

new needleful, as when commencing the work, putting the needle into the last hole the short end came out of, and sewing both ends down with the next stitches.

9. At the end of the work, fasten the thread by taking two or three stitches over each other *in the fold.*

Suggestions. — Hems should be begun and finished by neatly overhanding the ends of the fold. A narrow hem on stiff cloth, as on table linen, need not be basted. The seams of a garment should be sewed before hemming, to conceal the edges. Before turning the first fold, the end of the seam should be cut to avoid extra thicknesses and wear; when basting the hem, seams or stripes should exactly match. In sewing, to hold a wide hem easily, fold it over and over until it is a convenient width.

<small>What is a hem? How should the hem be folded? Where and how should it be basted? How many times should a wide hem be basted? How many times should a wide hem on woollen cloth be basted? Should there be a knot in the thread? How is the hem held? How should the needle point? Where is the needle inserted? How should the thread be drawn through? What is done with the end? How is the stitch made? How should the needle be held? How should the stitches be taken? In joining the thread, where should the end of the old thread be left? Where should the end be drawn? In starting with a new needleful of thread, where should the needle be put? What should be done with the two ends? In fastening, where and how should the stitches be taken? What should be done to the ends of a hem?</small>

RUNNING.

Running is done by passing the needle in and out of the material at regular intervals.

The rule for running is to take up two threads of the cloth and pass over two threads, but the light in the average school-room does not permit this, nor is it wise to strain the eyes trying to do so. The general principle is to pass over as much of the cloth as you take up.

RUNNING.

Materials. — No. 8 needle, No. 50 thread, and a half-yard strip of cotton cloth, doubled and basted.

Running. — Practise Drill No. 3 (page 15).

1. Make a small knot in the thread.
2. Hold the work in the left hand, between the thumb and cushion of the forefinger, as in Fig. 7 (page 15).
3. Sew directly below the basting.
4. Insert the needle between the edges of the seam, at the right-hand corner, and take the stitches (Fig. 21) over the cushion of the left forefinger, as in Drill No. 3 (page 15).

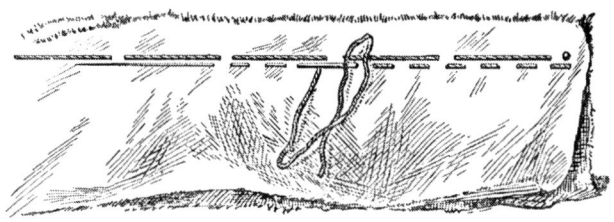

Fig. 21. — Showing the stitches, and the needle in position.

5. Fasten, by putting the needle through to the under side, and taking two or three stitches in the same place.
6. Join the thread, by sewing over the last stitches, or by making a knot and concealing it between the edges of the seam.

Suggestions. — To avoid puckering in running, begin at the right hand and smooth the seam between the left thumb and forefinger. Running is used for seams, which do not require great strength, also for tucking.

How is running done? What is the principle to be followed in running? How is the work held? Where are the stitches taken? Where is the needle inserted? How should the stitches be taken? How should the thread be fastened? How should the thread be joined? When is running used?

RUNNING AND A BACKSTITCH.

Running and a backstitch consists of two or more running stitches and a backstitch, taken alternately.

Materials. — No. 8 needle, No. 50 thread, and a half-yard strip of cotton cloth, doubled and basted.

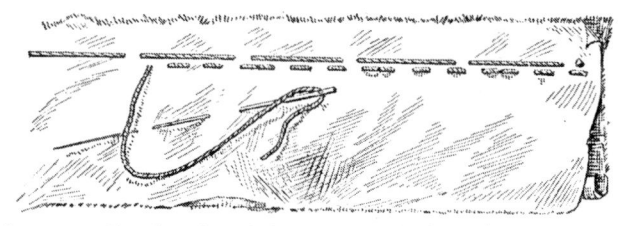

Fig. 22. — Showing the stitches, and needle in position for putting away the work.

Running and a backstitch. — 1. Begin as for running.

2. Take three running stitches.

3. Take one backstitch.

4. Repeat, which will cause every third and fourth stitch to meet (Fig. 22).

Suggestions. — Another method is to take three running stitches, making the third twice the length of the others, and then, putting the needle back to the middle of the last stitch, proceed as before. In this manner, the stitches on the right side resemble running, but on the wrong side there is a slight difference. Running and a backstitch is used when the seam needs to be sewed a little stronger than by running.

<small>Of what does running and a backstitch consist? When is running and a backstitch used?</small>

OVERCASTING.

Overcasting is done by taking loose stitches over the raw edge of cloth, to keep it from ravelling.

Materials. — No. 8 needle, No. 60 thread, and a stitched strip of cotton cloth.

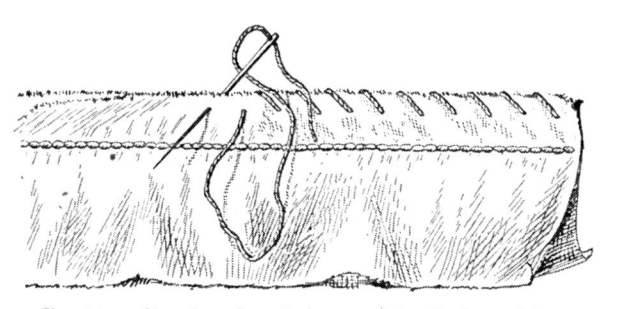

Fig. 23. — Showing the stitches, and needle in position.

Overcasting. — Practise Drill No. 4 (page 16).

1. Find one-eighth of an inch and one-fourth of an inch on the measure (page 13).
2. Place the thumb-nail on the cloth one-eighth of an inch below the raw edge. The stitches are to be of this depth, and twice as far, or one-fourth of an inch, apart.
3. Make a small knot in the thread.
4. Hold the work over the left forefinger, as in Fig. 8 (page 16).
5. Begin at the right-hand end of the seam.
6. Insert the needle one-eighth of an inch below the edge, and between the edges of the seam, in order to hide the knot.
7. Pointing the needle towards the left shoulder, take

the next stitch one-fourth of an inch to the left, and over both edges of the cloth.

8. Continue, taking up the same number of threads each time, being careful to make the spaces equal.

9. Do not draw the stitches tightly, but let them lie loosely over the edge (Fig. 23).

10. To fasten the thread, draw the needle nearly through the cloth where the next stitch should come. Turn over the cloth, withdraw the needle, and fasten the thread at this point, being careful that the stitches do not show on the right side.

11. To join the thread, make a small knot in the new thread, and put the needle between the edges of the seam, through the little hole, which was made when the needle was withdrawn.

Suggestions. — Before overcasting, take out the basting threads and trim the edges evenly. All seams whose edges ravel should be overcast, and, therefore, a selvedge seam does not need to be overcast. Overcasting is very difficult to do nicely. The above directions are for overcasting on underclothes, etc. In overcasting a dress waist, or any fine material, smaller stitches should be taken. A bias seam should be overcast from the broad part to the narrow, or with the grain of the cloth.

What is overcasting? How deep are the stitches taken? How far apart? How is the work held? At which end is the work begun? Where is the needle inserted? Why? How should the needle point? How far to the left should the next stitch be taken? How do you continue with the stitches? How is the thread fastened? How is the thread joined? What should be done before overcasting? When does a seam need to be overcast? How is a bias seam overcast?

OVERHANDING.

Overhanding is done by sewing closely over two edges of cloth. The edge of the cloth may be either a selvedge or a creased fold.

Materials. — No. 8 needle, No. 60 thread, and either two selvedge strips or two folded strips of cotton cloth, carefully basted together with even stitches, near the edge.

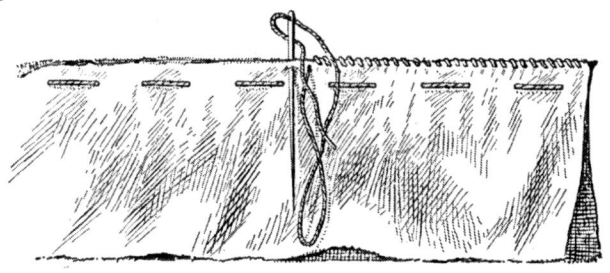

Fig. 24. — Showing overhanding stitches, needle in position.

Overhanding. — Practise Drill No. 5 (page 17).

1. Have no knot in the thread.
2. Hold the work horizontally *along the edge of the cushion of the left forefinger,* and around the end of the finger, as in Fig. 9 (page 17).
3. Pointing the needle towards you, insert it at the edge nearest you, taking up two or three threads of the cloth.
4. Carefully draw the thread through, leaving half-an-inch of the thread.
5. Hold the half-inch of thread down with the thumb, so that it may be sewed over by the first stitches (Fig. 26, *a*).

6. Pointing the needle towards the chest, put it through both edges, taking up as little of the cloth as possible.

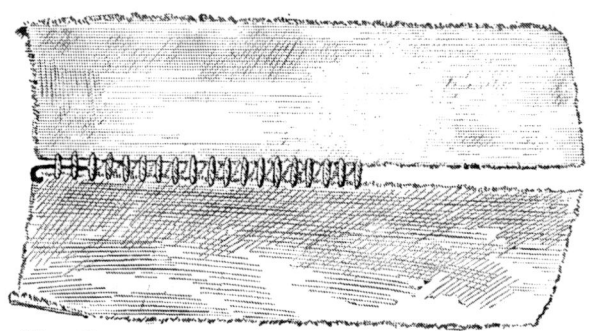

Fig. 25. — Showing how the stitches should look on the under side, with the seam opened.

7. Take the stitches *at the side of the cushion*, and make them close and even, having perpendicular lines on the under side of the seam (Fig. 25), and oblique lines across the edges (Fig. 24).

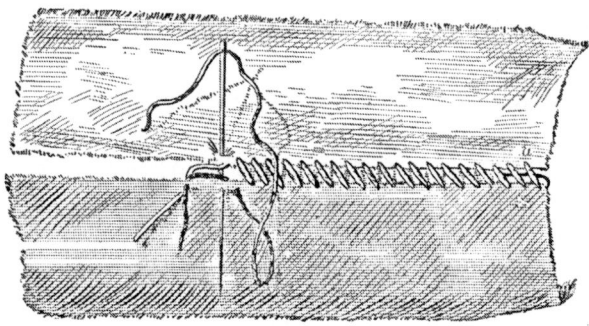

Fig. 26. — Showing, the edges of the seam being separated, how the end of the thread is fastened in beginning, how the stitches should look on the side towards you, and how to join the thread (the double line representing the old thread, and the black line the new thread).

OVERHANDING. 35

8. Joining the thread (Fig. 26). When the thread becomes too short for use, draw the needle through the further edge of the cloth, as in taking a stitch. Insert the needle at the opposite edge, one-fourth of an inch to the left, taking up one thread of the cloth. Draw the thread through, and remove the needle. Have no knot in the new thread. Pointing the needle from you, insert it at the hole where the old thread is hanging. Draw the thread through until about an inch is left, and hold the end under the thumb. Pointing the needle towards you, insert it at the nearest edge, exactly opposite the last stitch on the other edge. Hold the ends under the thumb, while the threads along the top are being overhanded; afterwards, cut the ends off.

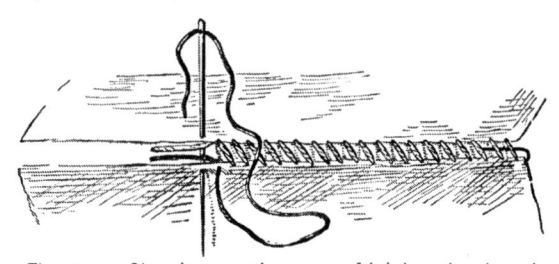

Fig. 27. — Showing another way of joining the thread.

The thread can also be joined as in Fig. 27. If preferred, a knot can be used by beginning back and sewing over a few stitches, and afterwards cutting off the knot.

9. Finish the seam by turning the work around, and overhanding back four or five stitches; this will fasten the thread securely.

10. When the seam is finished, draw out the basting thread, open the seam, and rub it first on one side and then on the other with the thumb-nail until it is flat.

Suggestions. — This stitch is sometimes called "top-sewing," also "over and over." The stitches should only be deep enough to hold, taking care to avoid making a ridge in the seam. The work will not pucker if the needle is pointed towards the chest, and the stitches are taken at the side of the cushion, not around the end of the finger. The necessity of taking the stitches properly is shown by overhanding two pieces of striped cloth. Either side of the sewing may be used as the right side. A seam in stiff material can be pressed open by holding it between the thumb and forefinger of each hand and rubbing.

How is overhanding done? How should the work be held? How and where should the needle be inserted? What should be done with the end of the thread? How are the stitches made? Mention one way of joining the thread. How should the seam be finished? What is done after the seam is finished?

GATHERING AND PLACING OF GATHERS.

Gathering is done by running the needle in and out of the cloth, passing over twice as much cloth as is taken up. It is used in joining a full part to a plain part, as an apron to a band.

Materials. — No. 8 needle, and a large blunt-pointed needle, No. 40 thread, and a piece of cotton cloth half-a-yard long and seven inches wide, hemmed at the sides and lower edge, and creased at the top.

Gathering. — Practise Drill No. 3 (page 15).

1. Find the middle of the creased edge, and mark the place by cutting a small notch in the edge (Fig. 28), or by making a cross-stitch with colored thread, one inch from the edge (Fig. 28).

GATHERING.

2. Use a single or double thread a little longer than the space to be gathered. A double thread helps to keep the gathers in place, but is more apt to knot than a single thread.

3. Make a good-sized knot in the thread, so that it cannot slip through the cloth.

4. With the *right* side of the cloth towards you, hold the work in the left hand, between the thumb and cushion of the forefinger, as in Fig. 7 (page 15).

5. Insert the needle on the wrong side, so as to conceal the knot, and through the hem to keep the knot secure.

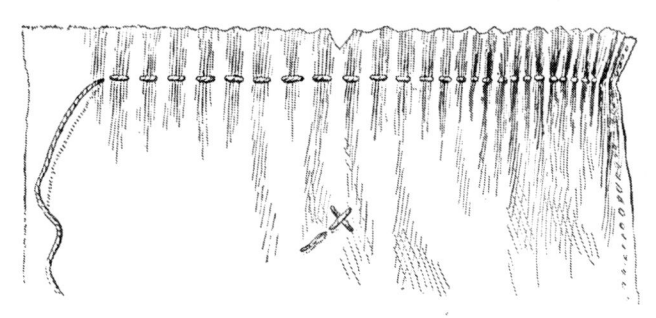

Fig. 28. — Showing the middle marked by a notch and by a cross-stitch, also showing gathering stitches.

6. Sew on the crease, taking several stitches before drawing the needle through.

7. Do not count the threads, but take up about half as many as you skip, *i.e.*, take up two threads and pass over four threads (Fig. 28).

8. If a knot, that cannot be untied, comes in the gathering thread, you will have to begin again.

9. When the seam is finished, remove the needle from the thread, and make a knot in this end of the thread.

10. Put a pin in vertically, close to the last stitch, taking up a few threads of the cloth.

11. Carefully draw up the thread, but not too tightly.

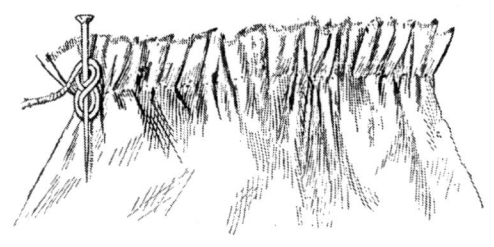

Fig. 29. — Showing the thread drawn up, and fastened around a pin.

12. Wind the thread over the top, and under the point of the pin a number of times, crossing the threads at the middle of the pin (Fig. 29).

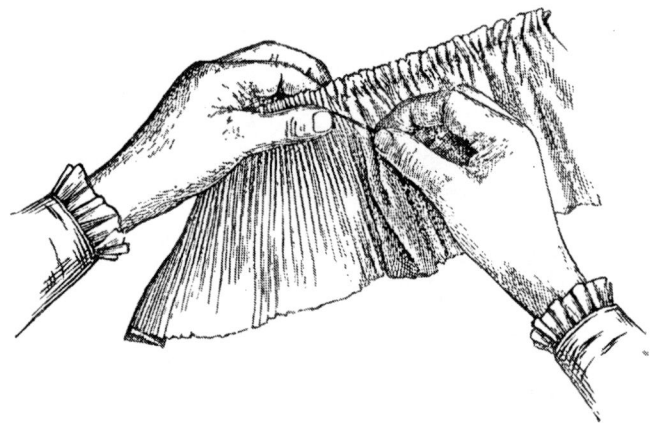

Fig. 30. — Showing the placing of gathers, with a large blunt needle.

Placing or stroking of gathers. — 1. With the right side towards you, begin at the *left*-hand edge.

GATHERING.

2. Hold the work between the left thumb and forefinger, as in Fig. 30, keeping the thumb below the gathering thread.

3. Put the point of the large needle under the gathering thread, holding it obliquely.

4. Press the needle towards the thumb, bringing the little plait under the thumb, and drawing the needle downwards.

5. Pinch it down tightly.

6. Continue in this way, putting the needle under each stitch.

Suggestions. — The part to be gathered should be divided into halves, quarters, or eighths, according to the width. When the part is only divided into halves, a notch may be avoided by beginning the gathering in the middle.

In placing, the eye of the needle can be used instead of a blunt-pointed needle. The upper part of the gathers often need a stroke of the needle. If a scratching sound is made in placing, marks are apt to be left, and the cloth torn. In thin, stiff materials, instead of placing, many stitches can be taken on the needle at once, and before drawing the needle through, push them close together; holding firmly, pull them into place and press them.

How is gathering done? When is it used? How is the cloth prepared? How long a thread should be used? What kind of a knot is required? How is the work held? How are the stitches taken? What is done after the seam is finished? How should the thread be drawn? How should the thread be wound? At which end should stroking begin? How is the work held in stroking? Where should the needle be put? What is done next?

DOUBLE GATHERING OR GAUGING.

Double gathering is done by making two rows of gathering, with the stitches of the second row directly under those of the first.

Materials. — No. 8 needle, No. 40 thread, and two pieces of cotton cloth, each half-a-yard long and seven inches wide, hemmed at the sides and lower edge.

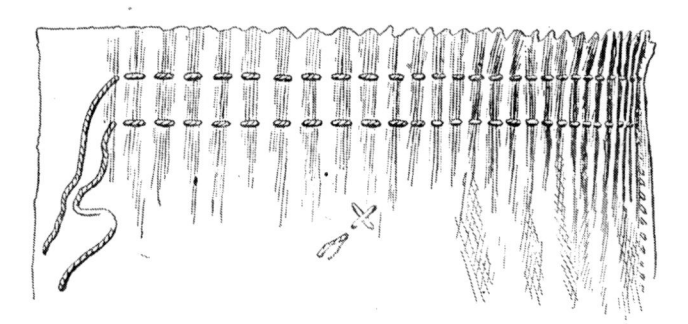

Fig. 31. — Showing double gathering on single material.

Double gathering on single material. — 1. Gather one-fourth of an inch from the raw edge.

2. When the end is reached, remove the needle, but do not draw up the thread.

3. Make a crease one-fourth of an inch below the gathering.

4. On the crease make another row of gathering, taking *each stitch directly below the one above it* (Fig. 31).

5. Remove the needle.

6. Take hold of both threads near the cloth, and gradually draw the gathers up to the required width.

Double gathering which is to be overhanded on to a binding.
— 1. Find the middle of the cloth, and mark it one and a half inches from the raw edge by a cross-stitch.

2. Crease one inch from the raw edge of the cloth, and let it remain folded.

3. Make two or more rows of gathering, the first row being *one-eighth* of an inch from the edge of the fold.

Suggestions. — When double gathering is used, there is no need of placing. Double gathering should be used on woollen materials, and quite long stitches be taken, if there is much fulness. Where the gathers are large, the second row can be easily made by closely drawing up the first gathering thread, and inserting the needle through many gathers at once.

How is double gathering done? How far from the edge should the first row, in single material, be made? In double material? How is the middle of the cloth marked for double gathering, that is to be overhanded to a binding?

SHIRRING.

Shirring is done by making several rows of running, parallel with each other.

Materials. — No. 8 needle, No. 40 thread, and a piece of cotton cloth half-a-yard long and twelve inches wide. The cloth should be folded lengthwise and basted.

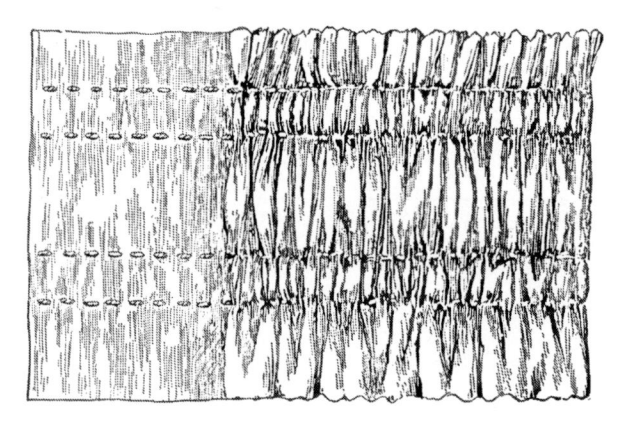

Fig. 32. — Showing shirring, and the stitches.

Shirring. — 1. Begin as in running.

2. Make the required number of rows at the desired distances from each other (Fig. 32).

3. Draw the gathers up on the threads, or by cords run between the rows.

How is shirring done? How are the gathers drawn up?

SCALLOPED EDGE.

A scalloped edge is used as a fancy heading for fulness.

Materials. — No. 8 needle, No. 60 thread, a strip of soft woollen cloth, and strong silk or thread to match in color.

Scalloped edge. — 1. Fold one of the lengthwise edges five-eighths of an inch from the edge, and baste close to the raw edge.

2. On the wrong side, and beginning at the right-hand end, mark the outer edge of the fold into inches with a colored pencil.

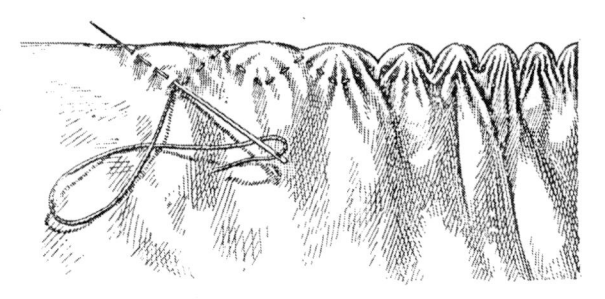

Fig. 33. — Showing a scalloped edge.

3. Half-an-inch below the outer edge of the fold, and beginning half-an-inch from the right-hand end, make another row of dots one inch apart. These dots should be midway between those of the upper row.

4. Make a good-sized knot, and inserting the needle at the upper right-hand dot, take small running stitches, slanting up and down, from dot to dot (Fig. 33).

5. Carefully draw up the thread every few inches.

For what is a scalloped edge used? What kind of stitches are taken?

HONEY-COMBING OR SMOCKING.

Honey-combing is drawing fulness together for ornamental effect.

Materials. — No. 8 needle, a piece of fine woollen cloth eleven inches long and three and a half inches wide, silk to match, and a red and a blue pencil.

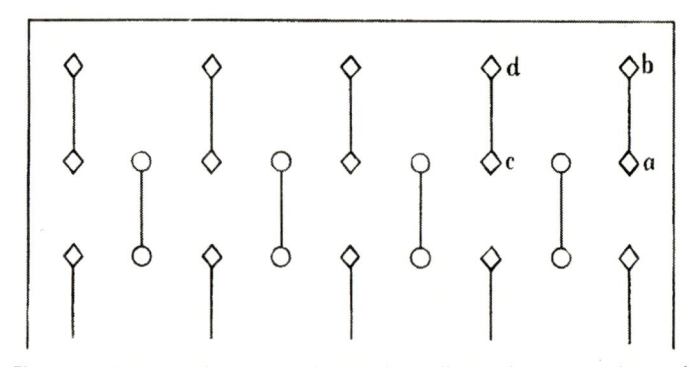

Fig. 34. — Showing how to mark the cloth, diamonds representing red dots, and circles blue dots.

Honey-combing. — 1. On the right side of the cloth, and beginning at one end, mark the entire length, as in Fig. 34, placing red dots in the place of diamonds, and blue dots in the place of circles.

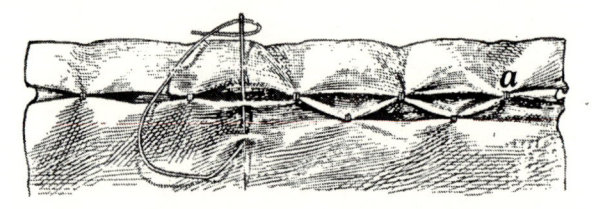

Fig. 35. — Showing honey-combing begun, needle in position

HONEY-COMBING. 45

2. Drawing the needle through from underneath at *a* (Fig. 34), take up a few threads of the cloth at *b* (Fig. 34), and fasten *a* and *b* together with two or three over and over stitches (Fig. 35, *a*).

3. Passing the needle underneath, bring it out at the next red dot (Fig. 34, *c*), and fasten *c* and *d* together.

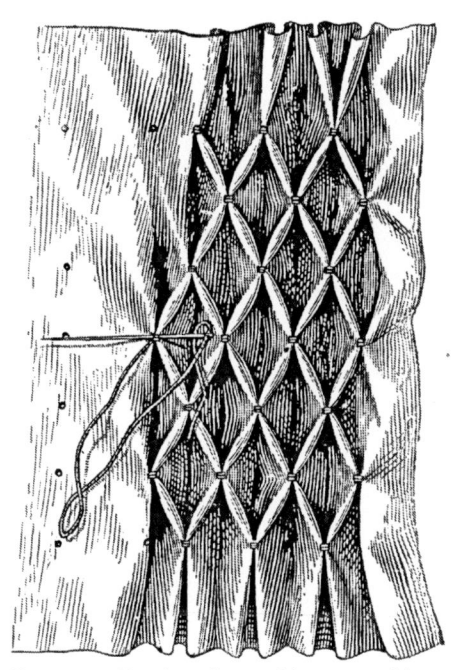

Fig. 36. — Showing diamond honey-combing.

4. Continue to the end of the row, fastening together the red dots which are connected in Fig. 34.

5. Beginning the second row at the right, fasten together, in a similar manner, the blue dots (circles, Fig. 34).

6. Work the third row as the first, and the fourth row as the second, and so continue (Fig. 36).

Suggestions. — In honey-combing, exactness is required in marking the spaces. Instead of colored pencils, the dots may be marked with thread or chalk. To keep the honey-combing in position, the outer edges should be fastened to a lining, after it is finished.

<small>What is honey-combing? Where is exactness required in honey-combing? How is honey-combing kept in position when finished?</small>

BINDINGS.

A binding or band is used to strengthen and cover the raw edges of a seam.

Binding No. 1. — Sewed by stitching and hemming.

Materials. — No. 8 needle, No. 50 thread, pins, scissors, and a piece of cotton cloth half-a-yard long and seven

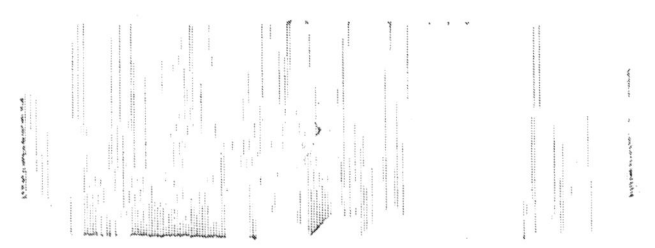

Fig. 37. — Showing the corners of the binding cut, and the middle of the edges marked by notches and a cross-stitch.

inches wide, notched in the middle, gathered and stroked (page 36); for the binding, a piece of cloth eight inches long and three inches wide.

Preparations. — 1. Find the middle of the band, and mark the place by cutting a notch (Fig. 37) at the edge of each side, or by taking a cross-stitch (Fig. 37) with colored cotton.

2. Cut off each corner of the band one-fourth of an inch deep (Fig. 37), to avoid having many thicknesses of cloth, when the corners are turned.

3. Loosen the gathering thread.

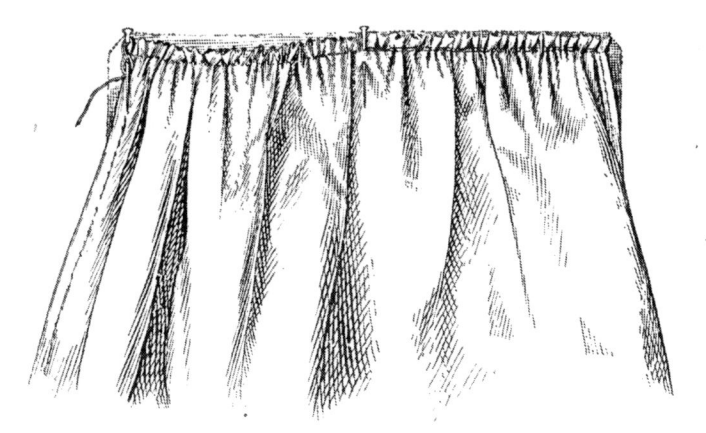

Fig. 38. — Showing half of the gathers basted and stitched.

4. Holding the wrong side of the gathered piece towards you, place the middle of the band at the notch in the middle of the gathers, and put in a pin vertically, to hold them together (Fig. 38).

5. Pin the ends of the gathers *one-fourth of an inch from each end of the band.*

6. Tighten or loosen the gathering thread, so that the length of the gathered edge exactly matches that of the band.

7. Fasten the gathering thread by winding it around the pin.

8. With the point of the needle adjust the gathers, so that the fulness is evenly distributed along the band.

9. Holding the gathers towards you, baste, with small stitches, a little above the gathering thread.

Stitching. — 1. Stitch the gathers to the band, exactly over the gathering thread, taking up only one gather at a time (Fig. 38).

2. Take out the pins, as you come to them.

3. If, when sewing, the gathering thread should be too short, loosen it by unwinding it from the pin.

4. When the band is stitched on, fasten the thread securely, cut off the gathering thread and take out the basting thread.

Hemming. — 1. Turn up the band, and crease the opposite edge and the two ends, one-fourth of an inch deep.

2. Cut off the corners of the gathers above the stitching.

3. Fold the band over to the line of stitching.

4. Pin the middle of the folded edge to the middle of the line of stitching.

5. Pin the ends, being careful to have the corners exactly together.

6. Baste the band down, keeping the edge of the fold *directly over* the stitching.

7. Overhand each end, beginning at the gathers.

8. Hem the band down, taking a stitch in each gather, *a little below* the stitching. Do not allow the stitches to show on the right side.

Suggestions. — A binding should be cut lengthwise of the cloth, when strength is required, or where much wear is coming, as on underclothing. A narrow binding for finishing a garment should be cut on the bias. The binding and gathering should be equally divided by notches, so that there may be no more fulness in one part than in another. If there are but few gathers, half-backstitching can be used instead of stitching. Great care should be taken to have the ends of the band neat; some prefer to turn the ends of the band under before stitching, others stitch the ends of the band together, before putting it on to the gathers.

Binding No. 2. — Sewed by setting-in the gathers.
Materials. — Same as for Binding No. 1.

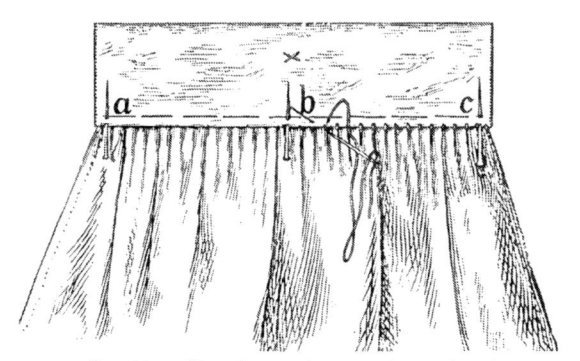

Fig. 39. — Showing gathers set into a band.

Preparations. — 1. Mark the middle of the band by a cross-stitch, and cut off the corners, as in Fig. 37.

2. Crease the four edges of the band.

3. Baste and overhand the ends, beginning at the corners.

4. Loosen the gathering thread.

5. Hold the right side of the gathers towards you.

6. Pin the middle of one edge of the band to the middle of the gathers, and exactly over the gathering thread (Fig. 39, *b*).

7. Pin the ends of the gathers, inside the ends of the band (Fig. 39, *a* and *c*).

8. Draw up or loosen the gathering thread, so that it is the same length as the band, and fasten around the pin.

9. Arrange the gathers with the needle.

10. Baste the band on, so that the gathering thread is covered.

Setting-in of gathers. — 1. Begin as for hemming, but make the stitch vertical on the side towards you.

2. Take up, close below the gathering thread, one gather and then a thread or two of the band (Fig. 39).

3. Take the next stitch by inserting the needle into the next gather (which should be directly under the place where the thread comes out of the band) and at the same time take up a thread of the band.

4. Take a stitch *in each gather*.

5. When this side is finished, fasten securely, and cut off the gathering thread.

6. Baste and sew the under part of the band in the same manner, taking care that the edge of the band corresponds exactly with the edge on the opposite side, in order that the band may not be twisted.

7. Do not let these stitches show on the right side.

Suggestions. — The shape of the stitch is like the letter N, as in overhanding, but the slant here is underneath, while in overhanding it is on the top. A binding is more easily sewed on in this manner, if there is a double row of gathering. To strengthen a binding, where a

BINDINGS. 51

button is to be placed, turn in one inch at the end of the band before folding it, and baste pieces of cloth on the under side where other buttons are to be placed ; at the button-hole end, turn in half-an-inch. Cut a button-hole in a binding nearer the gathers than the folded edge, so that the garment will be held in place firmly.

Binding No. 3. — Sewed by overhanding.

Materials. — Same as for Binding No. 1, with the larger piece of cloth gathered for overhanding to a binding (page 41).

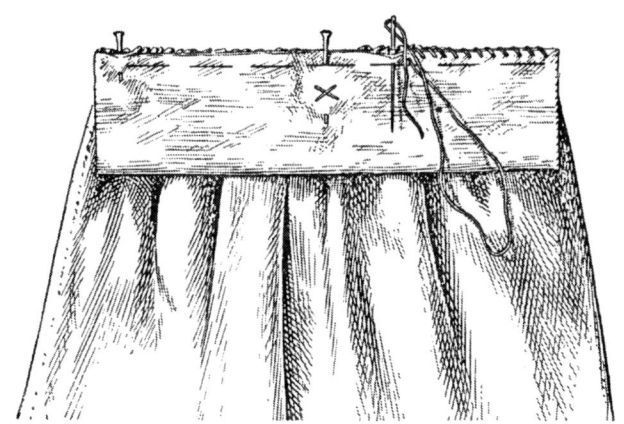

Fig. 40. — Showing gathers overhanded, with needle in position

Preparations. — 1. Mark the middle of the band by a cross-stitch, and cut off the corners, as in Fig. 37.

2. Crease the four edges of the band.

3. Double each end, and beginning at the corners, overhand both ends.

4. Baste the lengthwise edges together.

5. Pin the middle of the band at the middle of the right side of the gathers.

6. Pin the ends of the gathers and band together.

7. Draw up or loosen the gathering thread, until it is of the same length as the band, and fasten around the pin.

8. Arrange the gathers with the needle, and put in pins vertically every two inches.

Overhanding. — 1. Holding the band towards you, overhand the gathers to the band placing a stitch in each gather.

2. Take out the pins, as you come to them.

3. Fasten the gathering thread.

For what is a binding used? In what three ways can a binding be sewed on? How can the middle of the band be marked? What should be done to the corners of the band? Why? Where should the gathered piece and band be pinned together? What should be done to the gathering thread? How is it fastened? How should the gathers be adjusted? How basted? Where and how should the gathers be stitched? How is the band prepared for hemming? Where should the band be pinned? How is the band basted? What should be done at each end? Where should the hemming stitches be taken? When is a binding cut lengthwise? What should be done to the ends of a band before setting-in the gathers? How should the band be basted to the gathers? What letter should the stitch resemble? How can a band be strengthened, where buttons are to be placed?

FACINGS OR FALSE HEMS.

A facing is a fold applied to the edge of a garment for protection and finish, and has the appearance of a hem.

Materials. — No. 8 and No. 9 needles, No. 50 and No. 70 thread, pins, and two pieces of cotton cloth, one piece six inches long and four inches wide, the other piece, for the facing, six inches long and two inches wide.

Facing. — 1. Place the facing lengthwise on the piece of cloth, and pin the ends together.

2. Baste them together one-fourth of an inch from the edge.

3. Half-backstitch under the basting.

4. Take out the basting thread.

5. Fold the wrong sides together, and crease the cloth one or two threads beyond the seam, that the seam may not show on the edge.

6. Crease the opposite edge of the facing one-fourth of an inch deep.

7. Pin the ends of the cloth and facing evenly together.

8. Baste and hem.

Suggestions. — A facing which requires strength should be cut lengthwise. A narrow facing for a rounded edge, as the neck of a garment, should be cut on the bias, so that it may be stretched when being hemmed. A false hem can be used, when the material is not long enough to allow a hem.

_{What is a facing? What is its use? How should it first be sewed? How next? When can a false hem be used?}

BUTTON-HOLES.

A button-hole is a slit cut and worked in a garment to admit a button.

Button-Hole Stitch for Beginners.

Materials. — No. 8 needle, No. 40 colored thread, and a folded and basted strip of cotton cloth.

Button-hole stitch. — 1. Make a small knot in the thread.

2. Place the folded edge of the cloth across the cushion of the forefinger of the left hand, allowing the tip of the finger to show.

3. Hold the cloth firmly, keeping the end of the thumb near the folded edge.

4. *Work from you, instead of towards you.*

5. Draw the needle through from underneath, close to the folded edge of the cloth, which will bring the thread into position for the stitch.

6. Again insert the needle one-eighth of an inch from the edge, and exactly back of its first position.

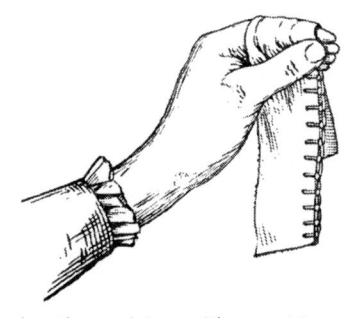

Fig. 41.— Showing the work in position, and button-hole stitches.

7. Let the needle remain half-way through the cloth, and pointing towards you.

8. Take the two threads at the eye of the needle, bring them towards you at the right of the needle, then under the point of the needle and from you (Fig. 44).

9. Pull the needle out, drawing the thread so that the twist or purl comes at the top of the folded edge of the cloth (Fig. 41).

10. One-eighth of an inch beyond take another stitch in the same manner.

BUTTON-HOLES. 55

11. So continue, making the stitches even.

12. When the thread becomes too short to use, turn to the other side of the cloth, and fasten lightly at the side of the last stitch, and away from the purl. After threading the needle, insert it beside of the last stitch, drawing it towards the purl. Turn to the right side, and draw the needle up through the last purl, and proceed with the button-hole stitch.

<small>What is the first thing to be done? Where should the folded edge of the cloth be placed? What part of the forefinger shows? How should the cloth be held? In which direction do you work? Where is the first stitch taken? Why? How far from the edge is the needle next inserted? How far through the cloth should the needle be brought? How should it point? What is done with the two threads? When the thread is drawn out, where should the twist or purl come? How much should be left between the stitches?</small>

BUTTON-HOLES.

Materials. — No. 8 needle, No. 40 colored thread, button-hole scissors, a medium-sized button, and a folded and basted strip of cotton cloth.

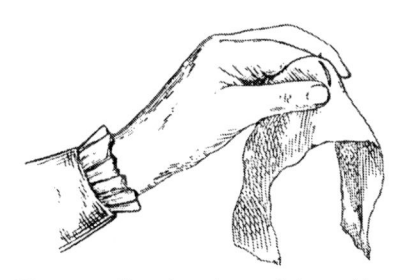

Fig. 42. — Showing the work in position.

The instructions are given in the following order : —

1. Cutting.
2. Barring.
3. Overcasting.
4. Button-hole stitch.
5. Finishing.
6. Joining the thread.

Cutting. — Cut the slit by a thread of the cloth, one-fourth of an inch from the folded edge, and a little longer than the diameter of the button.

Barring. — 1. Make a small knot in the thread.

2. With the folded edge from you, place the slit across the cushion of the left forefinger (Fig. 42).

3. Hold the slit *firmly* between the thumb and forefinger, and slanting as in Fig. 42.

4. Work from you, *beginning at the end farthest from the folded edge of the cloth.*

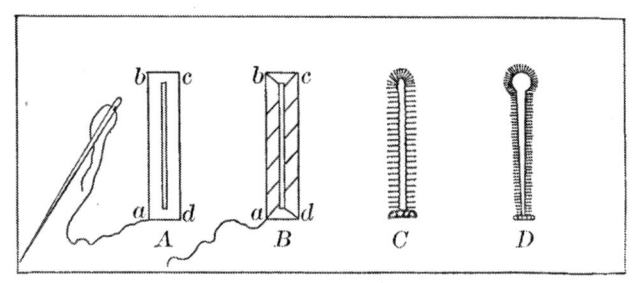

Fig. 43. — *A*, showing the barring of a button-hole; *B*, showing the overcasting of a button-hole; *C*, showing a finished button-hole; *D*, showing a button-hole on heavy cloth.

5. Draw the needle through from underneath, at the left of the slit, and three or four threads from the raw edge, *a* (Fig. 43, *A*).

6. Turn the cloth, so that the folded edge is towards you.

7. Insert the needle at *b* (Fig. 43, *A*), and bring it out at *c*, taking up three or four threads of the cloth at each side of the slit.

8. Again insert the needle at *b*, and bring it out at *c*. This makes a side and end barring.

BUTTON-HOLES. 57

9. Turn the cloth, and bar the other side and end in the same manner, *i.e.*, inserting the needle at *d*, bring it out at *a*, and repeat. This brings the needle to the starting point.

Overcasting. — 1. Hold the barring *tightly* near the edge of the slit.

2. Taking up three or four threads of the cloth, overcast one side, making the stitches over the barring and

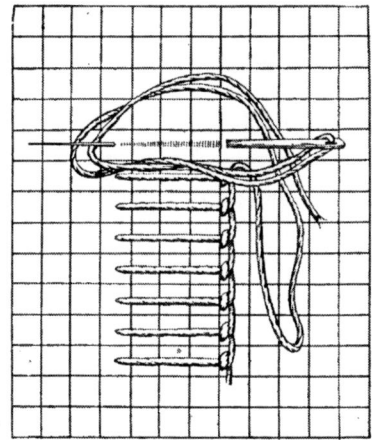

Fig. 44. — Showing button-hole stitches, enlarged, needle and thread in position. The straight lines represent the threads of the cloth.

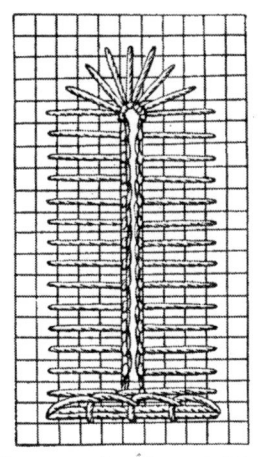

Fig. 45. — Showing a finished button-hole, enlarged.

one-eighth of an inch apart. Bring the needle at the last stitch into the corner, where the side and end barring meet, *b* (Fig. 43, *B*).

3. Turn the cloth, and take one overcasting stitch in the opposite corner, *c* (Fig. 43, *B*).

4. Overcast the remaining side and end in the same

manner, which will again bring the needle to the starting point.

Button-hole stitch or purl. — 1. Draw the needle halfway through at the left side, and one thread beyond, taking up about four threads of the cloth.

2. With the needle pointing towards you, take the two threads at the eye of the needle, and bring them towards you at the right of the needle, then under the point of the needle and from you (Fig. 44).

3. Draw the needle and thread out, at right angles to the slit, and so that the twist or purl comes at the top edge of the slit (Fig. 44). In making the purl, the thread will form the figure eight (8).

4. Continue in this manner, leaving a thread of the cloth between each stitch, and make the stitches even.

5. Take seven or eight stitches across the outer end (Fig. 45), drawing the purl towards the folded edge, and making either a square or round end. The greatest wear from the button comes here.

6. Holding the folded edge of the cloth towards you, work the second side until close to the end barring.

If, in taking the button-hole stitch, you fail to put the thread around the needle, the stitch can be picked up, by leaving a small loop, and, with the thread beyond it, passing the needle from underneath through the loop.

Finishing. — 1. Without turning the cloth, draw the needle down through the first button-hole stitch taken, bringing it up on the opposite side, where the side and end barring meet.

2. Draw this stitch so tightly as to bring the sides close together.

3. Make a barring exactly over the one already there, which will leave the thread at the left side.

4. Holding the thread under the left thumb, draw the needle under the two end barrings and over the thread, which will form the loop stitch.

5. Take another loop stitch in the middle of the barring and one in the right hand corner.

6. Draw the needle down through the cloth *close to the purl of the last loop stitch*, and fasten on the wrong side.

Joining the thread. — 1. If the thread should prove too short, put the needle through the slit, and turn to the other side of the cloth.

2. Fasten lightly beside the last stitch.

3. After threading the needle, insert it beside the last stitch, drawing it towards the purl.

4. Turning the right side towards you, draw the needle up through the last purl, and proceed with the button-hole stitch.

Suggestions. — On materials that ravel, make two parallel rows of stitching, and cut between the rows ; or the place may be dampened with glue and cut when dry. It is important to remember when making a button-hole, to work from you and begin at the end farthest from the edge. Try to keep the slit straight and not to press it out of shape. Some hold the slit horizontally on the forefinger. The distance that the button-hole is cut from the edge, depends upon the garment. The side of the garment in which the button-hole is made, is a matter of choice, but it is wise to decide upon one side and adhere to it. In woollen goods a triangle of a few threads of the cloth can be cut out of the end nearest the edge, or the end can be rounded.

The barring strengthens the button-hole and keeps it in place. If a great strain comes on the button-hole, put a double barring around.

Some prefer to overcast before barring, but the overcasting stitches are helpful in keeping the barring in place. When the overcasting is done first, take the overcasting stitches on the under or wrong side, thus securing the under edge, which is very apt to pull away in working. A material, that does not ravel, need not be overcast.

A button-hole can be finished by taking button-hole stitches in the loop, or on heavy goods by sewing closely over and over the barring. In a button-hole, where a strain comes on the sides, as in the front of a shirt, work both ends as in finishing an ordinary button-hole.

Always try to have the thread long enough to finish working the button-hole. For a very large button-hole, take a new piece of thread, when beginning on the button-hole stitch. On woollen cloth, button-hole twist should be used. On heavy goods, a cord is used instead of barring.

What is a button-hole? What is its use? Give the order in which the instructions for button-hole making are given.

CUTTING. — How should the slit be cut?

BARRING. — Where should the slit be placed and how held? In which direction do you work? At which end do you begin? Where is the needle inserted? What should be done next? What stitch is taken by following the directions for the end barring? How is the other side and end barred? Where will this bring the needle?

OVERCASTING. — How should the barring be held? How is the first side overcast? How is the end overcast? How is the needle brought to the starting point?

BUTTON-HOLE STITCH. — Where and how should the needle be inserted? How many threads of the cloth are taken up? In what direction should the needle point? What is now done with the two threads? How are the needle and thread drawn out? Where should the twist or purl come? What figure is formed by the thread, in making the purl? How many threads of the cloth should be left between the stitches? How should the outer end be worked? Where does the greatest wear come? How should the cloth be held in working the second side? How can a button-hole stitch be picked up?

FINISHING. — What is done with the needle? How should this stitch be drawn?

Where is the second barring made? How is the loop stitch formed? Where are the other loop stitches taken? Where should the needle be drawn, to fasten the thread?

JOINING THE THREAD. — What is done if the thread proves too short? After threading the needle, where should it be inserted? Where is it next brought?

Why is barring used? Is a material, that does not ravel, overcast? How long a thread should be taken?

BUTTONS.

A button is a catch of metal or other substance, by which a garment is fastened.

Materials. — No. 7 and No. 8 needles, No. 36 and No. 50 thread, a pin, a four-holed button, and a folded and basted piece of cotton cloth.

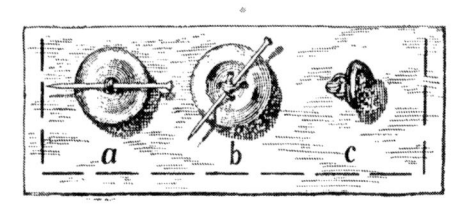

Fig. 46. — *a*, Showing the sewing of a two-holed button, pin in position; *b*, showing the sewing of a four-holed button, pin in position; *c*, showing the sewing of a boot-button.

Buttons. — 1. Make a pin-hole, where the button is to be placed.

2. Stitch with the fine needle and thread a very small circle around the pin-hole, or a cross at the pin-hole, to keep both sides of the cloth in place.

3. Having the coarse thread double, make a knot.

4. Draw the needle through the pin-hole from the upper side, to conceal the knot under the button.

5. Bring the needle partly through, close to the knot.

6. Place the button on the needle, and draw the needle and thread through.

7. Place the pin across the top of the button (Fig. 46, *b*), to lengthen the stitches; and take the first stitch across the button, at right angles with the edge of the cloth.

8. Sew securely through and through the holes, making a cross on the button, and two parallel lines on the wrong side of the cloth.

9. Remove the pin, which will loosen the stitches.

10. Inserting the needle from underneath, bring it out between the button and cloth, close to the centre of the button.

11. Wind the thread tightly around the stitches three or four times, to form a neck for the button; thus allowing room for the thickness of the button-hole.

12. Fasten the thread on the under side of the cloth.

Suggestions. — In sewing on a two-holed button, the stitches should be taken at right angles with the edge of the cloth (Fig. 46, *a*), to avoid stretching the end of the button-hole. A button with a loop, as a boot-button, should be sewed with the stitches taken parallel with the edge (Fig. 46, *c*); this will bring the wear on the loop of the button.

The button-holes should be made first. To mark the places for the buttons, lay the right sides of the garment together, and put pins through the outer ends of the button-holes; taking great care to have the pins exactly opposite the button-holes.

What is a button? What is its use? How should the place for a button be prepared? What kind of thread should be used? How should the needle be inserted? Why? What is placed across the top of the button? How is the button sewed on? How is the neck of the button formed? Why? How should the stitches be taken in sewing on a two-holed button? How on a button with a loop? How are the places for the buttons marked on a garment?

EYELET-HOLES.

An eyelet is a hole made and worked in a garment, to receive a small cord or the loop of a button.

Materials. — No. 8 needle, No. 40 thread, a stiletto, and a piece of cloth folded and basted.

Eyelet-holes. — 1. Pierce the cloth with the stiletto, breaking as few threads as possible.

2. Holding the hole tightly over the cushion of the left forefinger, work it over and over with very close, even stitches (Fig. 47, *a*).

3. When working on a line with the threads of the cloth, use great care to take the stitches close and deep enough.

4. Use the stiletto occasionally to keep the hole round.

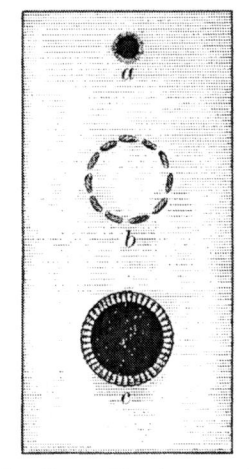

Suggestions. — To make a large eyelet-hole, mark the circle by twice running a thread around the desired size (Fig. 47, *b*); then carefully cut out the centre, turn the edge of the material under, and work the edge over and over or with button-hole stitches (Fig. 47, *c*).

Fig. 47.—*a*, Showing a small eyelet-hole; *b*, showing a large eyelet-hole, marked by running stitches; *c*, showing a large eyelet-hole finished.

On woollen materials, use silk or twist. An eyelet-hole can be worked with the button-hole stitch.

What is an eyelet-hole? What is its use? With what do we make an eyelet-hole? How should the eyelet-hole be held and worked? Where should care be taken?

HOOKS AND EYES.

A hook is a hard material, bent for holding or fastening. An eye is a small round catch to receive the hook.

Materials. — No. 8 needle, No. 40 thread, a medium-sized hook and eye, and two folded and basted pieces of cotton cloth.

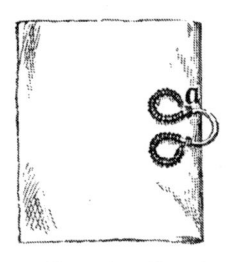

Fig. 48. — Showing a hook and eye sewed on.

Eyes. — 1. Make a knot in the thread.

2. Place the loop of the eye a little beyond the folded edge of one of the pieces of cloth.

3. Hold the loop firmly between the left thumb and forefinger.

4. Beginning at the further side, overhand closely the two circles of the eye (Fig. 48), being careful not to let the stitches show on the right side.

5. Take three stitches over each other at each side of the eye, near the edge of the cloth (Fig. 48, *a*).

6. Fasten very securely.

Hooks. — 1. Taking the other piece of cloth, lap the two pieces as desired.

2. Put the hook into the eye already sewed on, and place it in position.

3. Holding the hook firmly between the left thumb and forefinger, unfasten it.

4. Begin at the further side, and overhand closely the two circles (Fig. 48), being careful not to let the stitches show on the right side.

5. Overhand the under part of the hook, as far as the bend.

6. Fasten, by taking three or four stitches in the same place, at one side of the hook ; then run the needle to the opposite side, and again fasten. A great strain comes here, and it is necessary to fasten securely.

Suggestions. — If the eye is on a garment, where it is liable to show, cover it with button-hole or loop stitches. When sewing on hooks and eyes, use a strong thread or twist, and as fine a needle as possible.

<small>What is a hook? What is an eye? Where is the eye placed? How is it sewed on? How should the thread be fastened? What is done to the two pieces of cloth before sewing on the hook? Where is the hook placed before it is put in position? How is it sewed on? How is the thread fastened?</small>

LOOPS.

A loop is a catch made in a garment, to take the place of an eye.

Materials. — No. 8 needle, No. 40 thread, and a folded and basted piece of cotton cloth.

Loops. — 1. Make a knot in the thread.

2. Holding the folded edge of the cloth towards you, work from *left to right*.

3. Half-an-inch from the folded edge take three or four stitches one-fourth of an inch in length, and over each other (Fig. 49, *a*).

4. Holding the thread down with the left thumb, insert the needle under the backstitches, and over the thread (Fig. 49, *a*); being careful not to take up any threads of the cloth.

5. Draw the needle and thread towards you, so that the purl may come at the side of the loop towards you.

6. Fill the loop full of stitches drawn closely together.

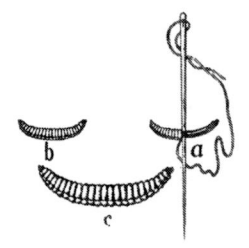

Fig. 49.—*a*, Showing the needle in position; *b*, showing a finished loop; *c*, showing a finished loop, enlarged.

7. At the right-hand end, draw the needle down through the cloth, *close* to the purl of the last stitch.

8. With a few stitches, overhand the underneath stitching, and fasten securely.

Suggestions.—In making a loop on a garment, the backstitches should be taken one-sixteenth of an inch beyond where the loop comes, when the garment is fastened. Button-hole stitches can be used instead of loop-stitches.

What is a loop? What is its use? In which direction do you work in making a loop? Where and how are the first stitches taken? How is the needle inserted? How is the needle drawn through? How many stitches should be taken in the loop? What is done to the underneath stitches?

GUSSETS.

A gusset is an angular piece of cloth, inserted in a garment, to strengthen and enlarge an opening.

Materials.—No. 8 needle, No. 60 thread, pins, scissors, and a piece of cotton cloth five inches square, hemmed on three sides; for the gusset a quarter of a four-inch circle of cloth.

Gussets. — 1. Find the middle of the side of the cloth not hemmed, and cut two inches and a half, by a thread.

2. Make a hem on each side, having it one-eighth of an inch wide at the top, and turned to a point at the bottom.

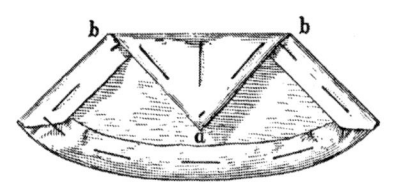

Fig. 50. — Showing the gusset folded over.

3. Find the middle of the rounded side of the gusset, and crease to the opposite corner.

4. Baste with even stitches along the crease.

5. On all the sides, fold and crease one-fourth of an inch.

6. Cut off all unnecessary thicknesses of cloth in the folds, and baste the folds down.

7. On each side, five-eighths of an inch from point *a* (Fig. 50), make a pin-hole; then fold and crease from pin-hole to pin-hole (Fig. 50, *b* to *b*).

Setting-in the gusset. — 1. With a small knot in the thread, draw the needle through from the wrong side of the gusset, at point *a* (Fig. 50).

2. Holding the *wrong side* of the cloth towards you, insert the needle from the right side, two or three threads from the end of the opening.

3. Holding the right sides together, overhand the gusset to the cloth, as far as the crease or point *b* (Fig. 50); fasten securely.

4. Overhand the other side in the same manner, beginning at point *a*.

5. Fold the gusset over on the crease.

6. Pin the end of the middle line of basting to the cloth a little below the opening (Fig. 51).

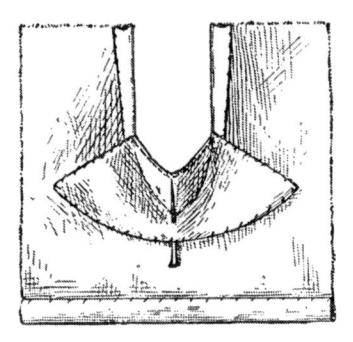

Fig. 51. — Showing the middle of the gusset pinned, and the finished gusset on the wrong side.

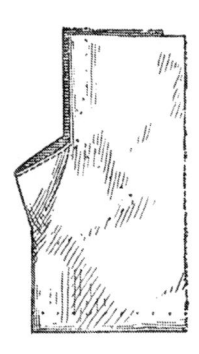

Fig. 52. — Showing the finished gusset on the right side.

7. Baste and hem the gusset to the cloth.

8. Make a row of stitching at the fold of the gusset, to strengthen it (Fig. 51).

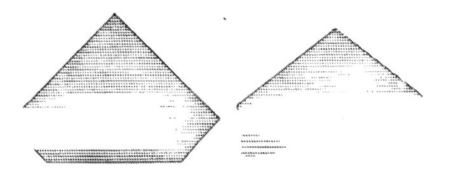

Fig. 53. — Showing other ways of cutting a gusset.

Suggestions. — The gusset can be made as large or small as desired; it can also be cut in different shapes (Fig. 53). An easy method of inserting a gusset is to cut a small square of cloth; fold and crease the edges; placing a corner at the end of the opening, overhand two sides; fold on the bias and hem the remaining sides over the overhanding stitches.

Gusset and facing. — 1. Make a paper pattern the desired size, having the gusset in the proportions of Fig. 54.

2. Fold the pattern at the dotted lines (Fig. 54), and place this edge on an exact *bias fold* of the cloth, which will bring the edge of the gusset on a line with a thread of the cloth.

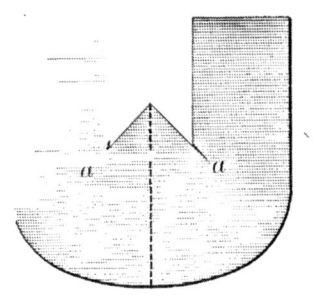

Fig. 54. — Showing the shape of a gusset and facing combined.

3. Cut the cloth by the pattern, and then cut in one-fourth of an inch to *a* (Fig. 54).

4. Make a narrow fold on the inner edges of the facing, and on the sides of the gusset make a fold turned to a point at *a*.

5. Fold the edges of the opening in the garment.

6. With the wrong sides together, overhand the gusset, and then the inner edges of the facing, to the opening in the garment.

7. Hem the opposite edges.

What is a gusset? What is its use? How should the hem in the opening be made? In setting-in a gusset, how is the point brought to the opening? What kind of stitches are then taken? What kind of stitches are used after folding the gusset?

PLACKET.

A placket is an opening made in a garment.

Materials. — No. 8 needle, No. 60 thread, and a piece of cotton cloth five inches square, hemmed on three sides.

Placket. — 1. At the middle of the side not hemmed, cut three inches by a thread.

2. Hold the wrong side of the cloth towards you.

3. At the left of the opening, make a hem turned to a point at the bottom, and one-eighth of an inch wide at the top.

4. At the right, make a hem three-fourths of an inch wide the entire length.

5. Turn to the right side of the cloth.

6. At the bottom of the wide hem make a horizontal crease *by a thread*.

7. On the right side of the opening, make a vertical crease *by a thread*, three-fourths of an inch from the edge.

8. Place the edge of the wide hem on this crease.

9. Holding the hem carefully, baste with small stitches, on the horizontal crease.

10. Make two rows of stitching, one a little below, and one a little above the basting.

What is a placket? When the wrong side is towards you, how wide a hem is made at the left? How wide at the right? How many rows of stitching are taken in tacking the hem?

TUCKING.

A tuck is a fold made and sewed in a garment for ornament, or that the garment may be lengthened when necessary.

Materials. — No. 8 and No. 9 needles, No. 50 and No. 90 thread, a sharp-pointed lead-pencil, and a piece of cotton cloth six inches square, having at one side an inch hem sewed exactly on a thread; for a measure, a stiff, smooth piece of paper or cardboard three inches long and half-an-inch wide.

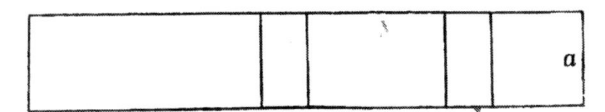

Fig. 55. — Measure for marking the tucks.

Tucking. — 1. Put the right-hand end of the strip of paper exactly to the right-hand end of the measure (Fig. 55).

2. One-eighth of an inch below the edge of the paper, with the lead-pencil, make dots corresponding to each line of the measure.

3. Hold the wrong side of the cloth towards you.

4. Half-an-inch from the right-hand edge of the cloth lay the paper on, with the end marked *a* (Fig. 55) *exactly* at the sewing of the hem.

5. Holding the paper and cloth even, put the large needle through each dot.

6. Move the paper two inches to the left, and prick.

7. Again move the paper two inches to the left, and prick.

8. Turn to the right side, and, holding the hem towards you, crease by a thread at the first horizontal line of dots.

9. Holding the crease to the light of the window, see if it is exactly by a thread.

10. Make a crease, by a thread, at the second, third and fourth lines of dots.

11. Fold the cloth down at the second crease.

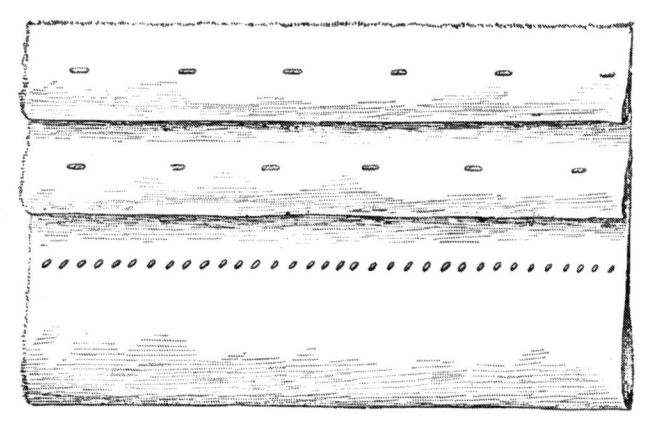

Fig. 56. — Showing the tucks basted.

12. Baste exactly by a thread on the first crease (Fig. 56).

13. Fold the cloth at the fourth crease, and baste on the third crease.

14. With the fine needle and thread, run each tuck close to the basting, taking up as little of the cloth as possible, and passing over twice as much.

Suggestions. — Tucks are sometimes made lengthwise of the cloth, and sometimes across the cloth. The width and distance apart are a matter of choice.

The chief difficulty is in measuring and folding them; when it is decided at what distance apart and what width the tucks are to be made, a paper measure can be made as follows.—Make a mark as far from the end of the paper, as the sum of the distance apart and the width of the tucks; make a second mark beyond the first mark, the width of the tucks; make a third mark as far from the second mark, as the sum of the distance apart and twice the width of the tucks; make a fourth mark beyond the third mark, the width of the tucks; continue as for the third and fourth marks. When two tucks have been made, the next can be easily marked by folding the wrong side together at the second tuck, and making pin-holes at the folds of the first tuck. The edge of one tuck may form the guide for measuring the next, though it is better to mark and baste all the tucks for a short distance. Narrow tucks, one-eighth of an inch apart, are neat and pretty, but must be made very carefully, as the difference of a thread is quickly noticed.

<small>What is a tuck? What is its use? How should the tucks be sewed? Which way of the cloth can they be made? What is the chief difficulty in making tucks?</small>

PLAITING.

A plait is a fold made in a garment, for fulness or trimming.

Materials.—No. 8 needle, No. 50 thread, pins, and a piece of cloth nine and a half inches long and four inches wide, with a narrow hem at the ends and lower edge.

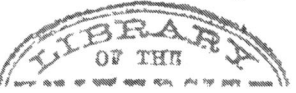

Plaiting.—1. On the raw edge of the cloth, with the right side towards you, measure one inch from the right-hand end, and mark it by cutting a small notch or inserting a pin vertically.

2. Mark every inch and a half to the left of this.

3. Fold the cloth at the first notch, and bring the fold to the edge of the hem.

4. Insert a pin in the middle of the three thicknesses o cloth.

5. Fold at the next notch, and bring it exactly to the underfold of the first plait.

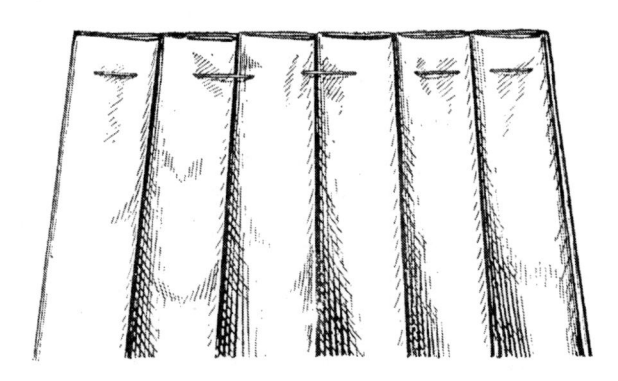

Fig. 57. — Showing basted plaits, half-an-inch wide.

6. Place a pin in the middle of the plait.

7. Fold and pin the other plaits in the same way.

8. Baste with even stitches, one-fourth of an inch from the edge (Fig. 57).

Suggestions. — Plaits can be laid either to the right or to the left. There can be spaces between the plaits, or they can meet, as in Fig. 57. If the plaits meet, the material must be three times the length that is desired when finished. Box-plaiting is made by beginning at the middle, and laying a plait to the right, and another to the left ; double box-plaiting is made by adding more side-plaits.

<small>What is a plait? What is its use? What different kinds of plaiting are there?</small>

FELLING.

A fell is a seam hemmed down to protect the edges.

Materials. — No. 8 and No. 9 needles, No. 50 and No. 80 thread, and two pieces of cotton cloth, each five inches long and two inches wide.

Fig 58. — Showing the seam basted.

Straight-way fell. — 1. Place the pieces of cloth together, with one edge one-eighth of an inch below the other, and baste a narrow seam (Fig. 58).

2. Sew the seam with a running and a backstitch.

3. Take out the basting thread, unfold the pieces of cloth, and lay the seam over, so that the wider edge will be uppermost.

4. Turn to the right side, and press carefully, exactly at the sewing of the seam.

5. Make a narrow hem (Fig. 59), tucking the ravellings under with the point of the needle.

Suggestions.— Hem a fell cut on the bias, with the grain of the cloth, or from the wider part to the narrow, as drawers from the top down. A fell can be made by

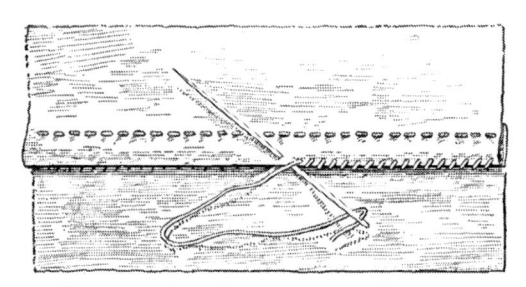

Fig. 59.— Showing the fell partly hemmed.

sewing it with the edges even, then pare one edge, being careful to have the right side of the sewing come on the upper side of the fell.

<small>What is a fell? What is its use? How are the pieces of cloth placed together? What should be the width of the seam? How should the seam be sewed? What is done, after the basting is removed? What is done next? How is a fell, cut on the bias, hemmed?</small>

FRENCH SEAM.

A French seam is a neat manner of joining materials that fray.

Materials.— No. 8 needle, No. 60 thread, scissors, and two pieces of calico, each five inches long and two inches wide.

French seam.— 1. Place the wrong sides of the calico together.

2. Baste one-eighth of an inch from the edge.
3. Run directly under the basting.

4. Cut the ravellings from the edges of the seam.

5. Turning the wrong side of the calico towards you, fold the right sides together, and crease at the sewing of the seam.

6. Baste, so that the raw edges are enclosed.

7. Half-backstitch the seam, being careful that no ravellings can be seen on the right side.

Suggestion. — Trimming can be put on in this manner, having the seam very narrow.

What is a French seam? Which sides of the cloth should be placed together? How wide a seam should be made? With what kind of stitches should the seam be finished?

FRENCH HEM ON DAMASK.

French hemming is used in hemming table-linen.

Materials. — No. 9 needle, No. 70 thread, and a strip of cotton cloth or table-linen.

French hem. — 1. Crease a narrow hem.

2. Holding the wrong side towards you, fold and crease the cloth, so as to make it even with the first fold of the hem.

3. Proceed as in overhanding.

SLIP OR BLIND-STITCH.

A slip or blind-stitch is used to fasten a hem lightly.

Materials. — No. 9 needle, No. 70 thread, and a strip of cotton cloth.

Slip or blind-stitch. — 1. Fold and crease a hem half-an-inch wide.

2. Baste about a fourth of an inch from the edge.

3. Make a small knot in the thread.

4. Conceal the knot by drawing the needle through the under part of the fold, one-eighth of an inch from the end.

5. Take up one or two threads of the cloth, and before drawing the needle through, take up one-fourth of an inch of the edge of the fold.

6. Continue in this manner, being careful not to draw the thread tightly.

7. Fasten securely.

Suggestions. — This stitch is used for sewing hems on woollen cloth, where it is desired to conceal the stitches. Trimmings of silk and velvet are often put on with this stitch.

<small>For what is a slip or blind-stitch used? How are the stitches taken?</small>

EDGINGS AND RUFFLES.

An edging is a trimming on the border of a garment.

Lace Edging.

Lace edging is made of fine threads woven into a net.

Materials. — No. 9 needle, No. 70 thread, pins, half-a-yard of inch-wide lace, and a piece of cotton cloth six inches long and four inches wide, with a narrow hem at the ends and upper edge, and an inch hem at the lower edge.

Lace edging. — 1. Holding the scalloped edge towards you, make a narrow hem at the right-hand end of the lace.

EDGINGS AND RUFFLES.

2. Holding the right sides of the lace and cloth together, place the hemmed end of the lace at the top edge of the upper left-hand corner of the cloth.

3. Holding the lace loosely, lightly overhand the edges to within a fourth of an inch of the corner.

4. Run the needle in and out of the cloth, to keep it temporarily secure.

5. Pin the lace at the corner.

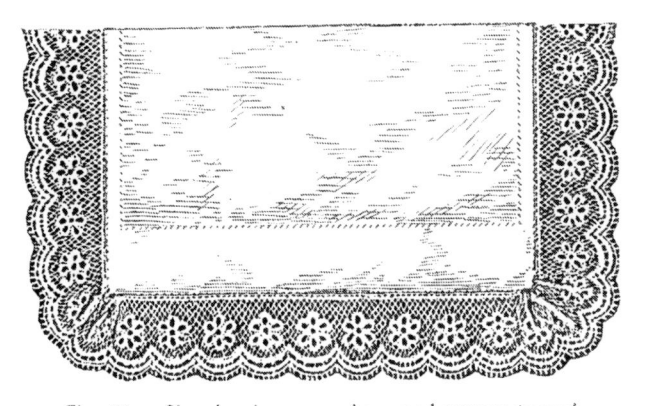

Fig. 60.—Showing lace sewed on, and corners turned.

6. Measure the width of the lace, and leaving twice the width, pin again at the corner.

7. One-fourth of an inch beyond the corner, pin the lace to the cloth.

8. Run a gathering thread in the edge of the lace, from the overhanding to the last pin.

9. Overhand around the corner, bringing the fulness as much as possible at the corner (Fig. 60).

10. Turn the other corner in the same manner, and finish by hemming the end of the lace.

Suggestions. — Lace can be sewed on full by dividing the lace and the edge to which it is to be sewed, into halves, quarters, etc.; and running a gathering thread through the edge of the lace, before basting it on. In turning corners, it is better to leave a little more than twice the width of the lace, as there must be enough on the outer edge, to prevent the lace from hooping. With wide lace, leave more than one-fourth of an inch on each side of the corner, for the fulness of the lace.

When measuring for the quantity of edging needed, allow enough for the corners. When the ends of the lace meet, join by a fell.

HAMBURG EDGING.

Hamburg edging is an embroidered edge, made by machinery. It can be sewed on, when no fulness is required, by a fell (page 75), a French seam (page 76), a facing (page 52), or by overhanding; when fulness is required, by a facing (page 52), or by whipping (page 82).

When much wear will come on the edging, it is advisable to overhand it, as it can then be easily removed; the raw edge of the Hamburg should first be overcast with very *fine* thread. The corners should be turned, and the ends sewed, as with lace.

RUFFLES.

Ruffles are made of various materials, and are plaited, gathered, or whipped.

Materials. — No. 8 and No. 9 needles, No. 40, No. 70, and No. 80 thread, pins, scissors, and a piece of cotton cloth six inches long and three inches wide, hemmed at the ends and upper side; for the facing, a piece of cloth six inches long and one and a half inches wide ; for the ruffle, a piece of cambric nine inches long and two inches wide, with a very narrow hem at the ends and lower edge.

A ruffle faced on. — 1. Mark the raw edges of the ruffle and the cloth, by notches, into halves and quarters. Also mark the middle of the facing by a notch.

2. Gather the ruffle.

3. Place the right sides of the cloth and ruffle together, and pin at the corresponding notches.

4. Draw up the gathering thread, and fasten around the pin.

5. Adjust the gathers, and run exactly on the gathering thread.

6. Pin the middle and ends of the facing to the ruffle, and baste.

7. Turn the other side towards you, and half-backstitch close below the running stitches.

8. Take out the basting threads.

9. Turn the facing over and crease it carefully at the seam.

10. Baste and hem the opposite edge of the facing.

Suggestions. — A heading on a ruffle can be made by folding the required width for the heading, and gathering it, making one or more rows as desired. The fulness of the ruffle depends upon the material ; a narrow cambric ruffle should be about one and a half times the length of the part to which it is to be sewed. In making a ruffle of more than one breadth, the ends should be joined neatly before hemming or gathering.

What is an edging? Of what is lace edging made? How should the lace be held in overhanding? What allowance for fulness should be made in turning a corner? How should lace be sewed on, when fulness is required? What is Hamburg edging? In what ways can it be sewed on, when there is no fulness? When fulness is required? From what are ruffles made? What is first done to the ruffle, the cloth, and the facing?

WHIPPING.

Whipping is forming gathers by overcasting a rolled edge of fine material, and drawing up the thread.

Materials. — No. 6 and No. 8 needles, No. 40 and No. 60 thread, pins, scissors, a strip of paper, and a piece of cotton cloth six inches long and four inches wide, with a narrow hem on the ends and upper edge, and an inch hem on the lower edge ; for the ruffle, a piece of plain cambric, twelve inches long and two inches wide, with a narrow hem on the ends and one side.

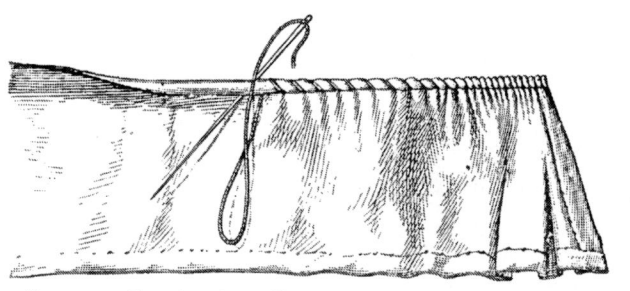

Fig. 61. — Showing the rolling and overcasting of the ruffle.

Whipping. — 1. Practise rolling tightly the edge of the piece of paper. It must be rolled, not folded.

2. Divide the edge of the inch hem, and the raw edge of the cambric, into halves and quarters, and mark, one inch from the edge, by cross-stitches.

3. Trim the ravellings from the raw edge.

4. Hold the wrong side of the cambric towards you.

5. Beginning at the right-hand corner, roll the first half-inch of the cambric towards you, between the thumb and the forefinger of the left hand.

6. Take the coarse needle and thread, and make a small knot.

7. Inserting the needle at the corner, under the roll, take one or two stitches, to fasten the end.

8. Hold the end of the roll between the right thumb and forefinger, and, placing the cambric between the third and little finger of the left hand, draw *tightly*.

9. Pressing the left thumb against the forefinger, rub an inch of the edge upwards and downwards, until a small, firm roll is made.

10. Overcast, as far as the cloth is rolled tightly, inserting the needle under the roll (Fig. 61).

11. Draw up the thread, holding it on a line with the raw edge. If the roll is *small*, and the stitches are taken loosely and at *regular intervals*, the ruffle will draw easily on the thread.

12. Continue, rolling and whipping an inch or two at a time.

13. Placing the right sides of the ruffle and hem together, pin the divisions of the ruffle to the divisions of the hem.

14. Draw up the ruffle to the length of the hem, and wind the thread around the pin.

15. Holding the ruffle towards you, overhand, inserting the needle in each fold of the whipping, so that the thread will lie between the folds (Fig. 62).

16. Fasten both the whipping and the overhanding thread.

Suggestions. — The fingers should be perfectly clean, to prevent soiling the work. In whipping, some prefer to take hemming stitches instead of overcasting stitches. A ruffle, for whipping, should be twice the length of the part to which it is to be sewed ; it is sometimes advisable to make it more than twice as full. A ruffle cut across the cloth whips easier than one cut lengthwise. A fine material whips more readily than a coarse one. Ruffles should be cut by a thread, which can be done by tearing, and then trimming the edges.

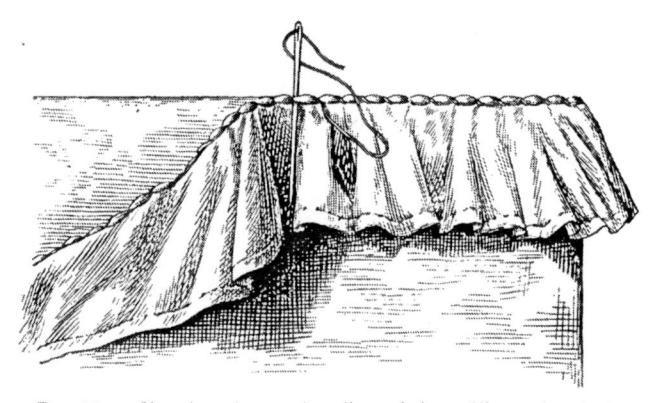

Fig. 62. — Showing the overhanding of the ruffle to the cloth.

It is best to use short lengths of thread, as a great strain comes, when the ruffle is drawn. In making a long ruffle, have a thread for each division, and measure as you draw the thread. The thread will draw easier, if a large needle is used. When corners are to be turned, allow extra fulness, so that the ruffle will lie flat (page 79). In overhanding a ruffle, the garment can be held towards you, but, if the whipping thread should prove too short, there is no way to lengthen it ; while, if the ruffle is held towards you, the thread can be drawn up or lengthened.

What is whipping? In whipping, which side of the ruffle should be held towards you? How do you begin? What kind of a needle and thread should be used? How is the roll held? How rolled? What is done next? How is the thread drawn? How continue? How is the ruffle sewed on to the hem?

STOCKINET DARNING.

Stockinet darning is used in filling in a hole with thread, so as to supply the part that has been destroyed; or in strengthening a place which shows signs of weakness.

PRACTICE IN WEAVING.

Materials. — A long-eyed needle, a knot of split zephyr, a sharp-pointed lead-pencil, and a two and an eighth inch square of cardboard.

Lattice-work. — 1. Turn to the measure (page 13).

2. On one side of the cardboard half-an-inch from the end, and one-fourth of an inch from the edge, make a dot with the pencil.

3. On a line with this dot, make nine more dots exactly one-eighth of an inch apart.

4. Mark the opposite side with dots *exactly parallel* to the other dots.

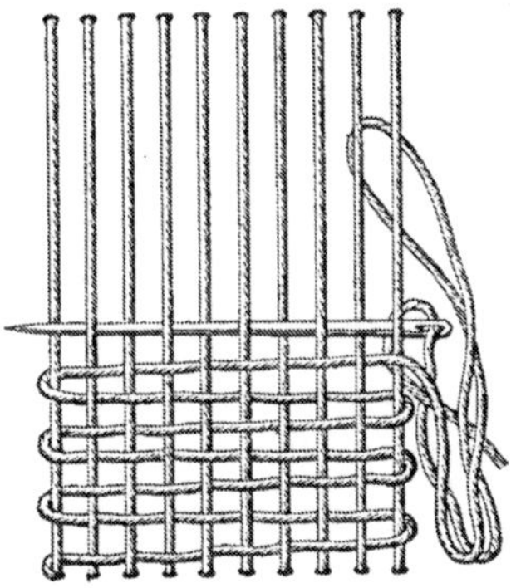

Fig. 63. — Showing the weaving or lattice-work of threads over cardboard.

5. Make a knot in the zephyr and work across the cardboard from dot to dot (Fig. 63), having the stitches on the under side one-eighth of an inch long.

6. Weave across these threads by taking up and passing over a thread alternately (Fig. 63). Take a number of threads on the needle at once.

7. Make the second row by taking up those threads, which were passed over before.

8. When the row is finished, leave a short loop of the zephyr at the opposite end, and holding it firmly, draw the zephyr until it is straight.

9. Continue in this manner, always taking up the threads passed over in the previous row.

Suggestion. — Coarse canvas can be used instead of cardboard, and in the place of zephyr, a small cord or coarse thread can be used.

STOCKINET DARNING.

Materials. — A long-eyed needle, No. 7 needle, No. 50 thread, scissors, a small spool of embroidery silk, a piece of cardboard or heavy paper three inches long and two and a half inches wide, and a piece of woollen stockinet, cut four inches lengthwise by a rib of the stockinet, and three inches and a half across.

Stockinet darning. — 1. Place the cardboard on the wrong side of the stockinet, leaving half-an-inch at each side to be folded over the cardboard.

2. Baste one of the lengthwise edges of the stockinet, having it folded *exactly* by a rib.

3. Drawing the stockinet smoothly across, fold the opposite side by a rib, and baste.

4. Fold and baste the ends.

5. In the centre of the stockinet, cut a circle, three-fourths of an inch in diameter.

6. Holding the stockinet lengthwise, begin at the right side, half-an-inch from the edge of the circle (Fig. 64, *a*).

7. Pointing the large needle from you, take two stitches, leaving half-an-inch of the end of the silk to be cut off afterwards.

STOCKINET DARNING.

8. With the needle pointing towards you, make the next row of three stitches, taking up the threads of the stockinet, that were passed over in the preceding row.

9. So continue, making each row a little longer at both top and bottom, as in Fig. 64, till the centre of the circle is reached; then decrease in the same proportion (Fig. 64).

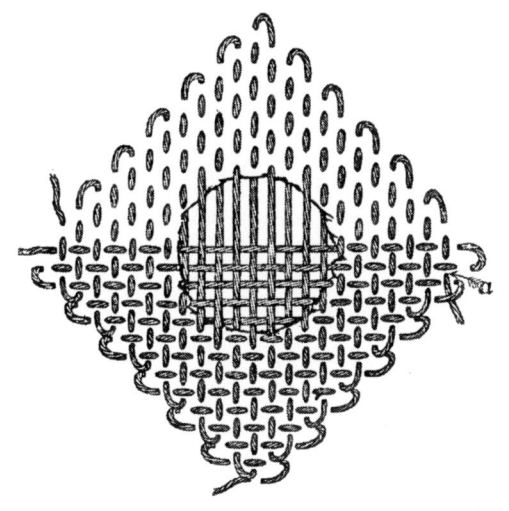

Fig. 64.— Showing a hole cut, and partly darned.

10. Be careful to put the needle through the loops of the stockinet, at the edge of the circle.

11. Cross the darn in the same manner, making perfect lattice-work, (Fig. 64).

Suggestions. — The stockinet is put on the cardboard to keep it in place while being worked, and silk is used that the stitches may be easily seen, and also that the lesson may be interesting. In mending a stocking, hold the work across three fingers of the left hand. A darning ball can be used, which prevents the fingers from being pricked, but it is apt to stretch the stocking and the darn. The darning can be done on either side of the stocking, and should be worked as far as the stocking shows signs of weakness; it should first be worked vertically and parallel to the ribs of the stocking. Loops of about one-sixteenth of an inch can be left at each end, to provide for shrinkage; stretching the darn slightly, when it is finished, will take up these loops.

The edge of a darn must never be made on one thread, as a single thread is not strong enough to bear the strain; a diamond or oval shape is better. It is wise to darn a thin place before a hole appears. In mending a large hole, draw out the rough ends, and, using a fine needle and thread, bring the loops or threads as near as possible to their proper position. To retain the proper shape of a large darn, begin the crossing at the middle instead of the end. The darning yarn should correspond in color and quality to the stocking. If too coarse a yarn is used, a hard bunch is made.

For what is stockinet darning used? How should the stockinet be held? Where should the darning begin? How is the first row made? How is the second row made? How continue? What care should be taken at the edge of the circle? How should a darn be crossed? In mending a stocking how should the work be held? What are the best shapes for darning?

GRAFTING.

Grafting is joining two pieces of stockinet in such a manner, as to render the joining invisible.

Materials. — A long-eyed needle, two pieces of coarse stockinet, and yarn the quality and color of the stockinet.

Grafting. — 1. Ravel the two edges that are to be joined, until the loops are perfectly even and clear.

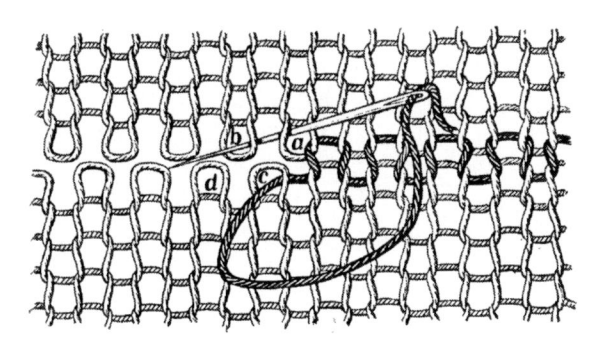

Fig. 65. — Showing grafting stitches, and needle in position.

2. Place the edges together, so that the loops of one are exactly opposite the corresponding openings of the other (Fig. 65).

3. Holding the right side towards you, work from right to left.

4. Fasten the end of the yarn, by darning it in and out on the wrong side of the stockinet.

5. Inserting the needle in an upper loop (Fig. 65, *a*), bring it out in the next loop (Fig. 65, *b*).

6. Inserting the needle in the under loop (Fig. 65, *c*)

opposite the last upper loop, bring it out in the next loop (Fig. 65, *d*).

7. Continue, taking two upper loops, then two under loops, using one new loop each time, which will cause the needle to be inserted twice in each loop.

8. Fasten the yarn, by darning it in and out on the wrong side.

Swiss-darning. — The stitches in Swiss-darning are taken in a manner similar to grafting, and are worked over the stitches in the stockinet, to strengthen a thin place.

Suggestions. — A patch in stockinet can be put in almost invisibly as follows : cut a square or oblong hole in the stockinet, carefully, by a thread, and ravel the sides until the loops are even ; cut the patch, by a thread, the exact size of the hole, and clear the loops ; graft in the top and lower edges, and Swiss-darn the side edges together, working over four or five stitches at each side of the joining.

<small>What is grafting? What is first done? How are the edges placed together? How are the stitches taken? How are the stitches taken in Swiss darning?</small>

STOCKING-WEB STITCH.

Stocking-web stitches are used for filling in a hole in stockinet, so as to present the same appearance as the woven stockinet, and are made on a foundation of strands.

Materials. — A long-eyed needle, No. 7 needle, No. 40 thread, a piece of coarse stockinet three inches square, yarn to match in color and quality, and a piece of cardboard two inches square.

STOCKING-WEB STITCH.

Stocking-web stitches. — 1. In the centre of the stockinet, cut carefully, by a thread, an inch square.

2. Ravel the edges until the loops are clear and even.

3. With the wrong side of the stockinet to the cardboard, fold over the edges and baste carefully.

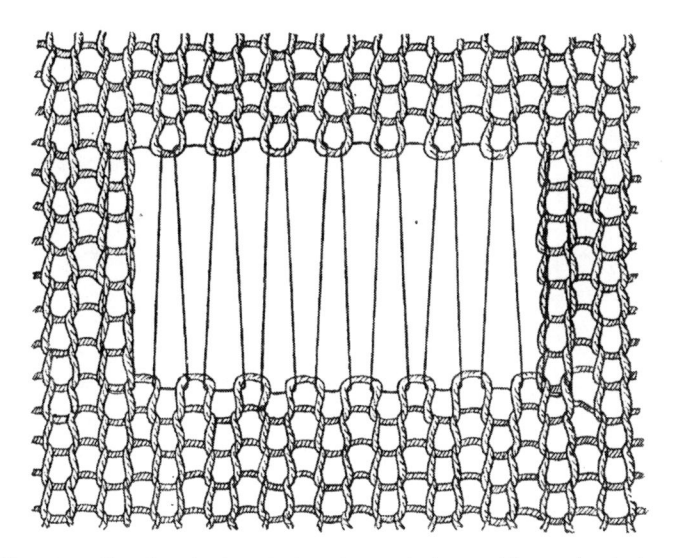

Fig. 66. — Showing the foundation of strands for stocking-web stitches.

4. With the fine needle and thread, connect the upper and lower loops, as in Fig. 66.

5. Hold the ribs of the stockinet vertically.

6. Having the coarse needle threaded with the yarn, insert it one or two loops to the right of the lower row, and one row above (Fig. 67, *a*).

7. Swiss-darn (page 90) over these stitches, and work across the strands with a stitch similar to grafting, insert-

92   SCHOOL NEEDLEWORK.

ing the needle between the strands in beginning and finishing the loop (Fig. 67).

8. Finish the row by Swiss-darning over two or three loops beyond.

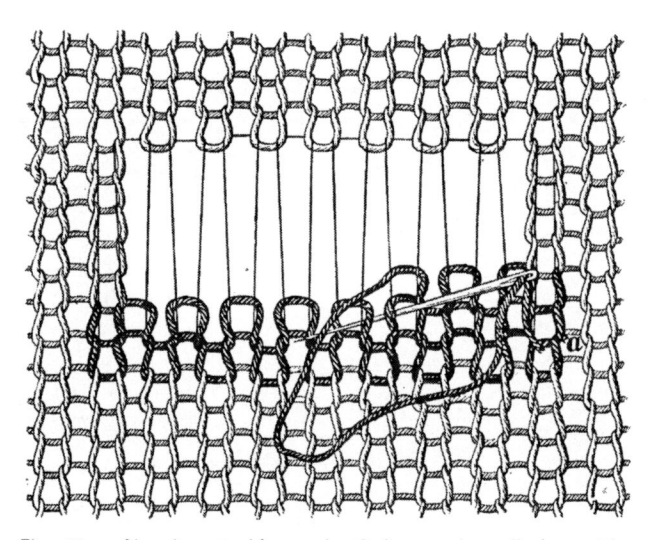

Fig. 67. — Showing stocking-web stitches, and needle in position.

9. Turn the work around, and one row above, work back in a similar manner.

10. Continue working up the strands, and finish by grafting the last row of loops made, to the loops of the stockinet.

For what are stocking-web stitches used? On what are they made?

CLOTH DARNING.

Cloth darning is used to strengthen worn places, or to draw together the edges of a tear or cut.

STRAIGHTWAY–DARN.

Materials.— No. 9 needle, No. 80 red, blue and pink thread, and two pieces of cotton cloth, each three inches and a half square.

— — — — — — — — — —· Pink thread.
·— — — — — — — —· Blue thread.
— — — — — — — — — —· Pink thread.

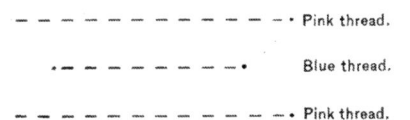

Fig. 68.— Showing the cloth prepared by running lines, for practice in darning a straightway-tear; the blue thread representing the tear.

Straightway-tear.— Darned with vertical stitches. A blue thread represents the tear.

1. Crease across the middle of one of the squares of cloth.
2. Leaving an inch and a fourth at each end, make a running on the crease, with the blue thread (Fig. 68).
3. Make two creases, one, one-fourth of an inch above; and one, one-fourth of an inch below the running.
4. Leaving an inch at both ends, make a running on each crease, with pink thread (Fig. 68). (The pink threads are boundary lines for the stitches).
5. Hold the tear over the cushion of the left forefinger.
6. Threading the needle with red thread, insert it at the right of the lower pink line (Fig. 69, *a*).
7. Take six running stitches upwards, bringing the

needle out a little below the upper pink line (Fig. 69, *b*) and leaving an end of the thread to be cut off later.

8. Finish the row, by inserting the needle above the line; draw it through below the line for beginning the next row.

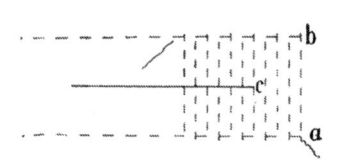

Fig. 69.—Showing the tear partly darned with vertical stitches.

9. Taking up the threads of the cloth, which were passed over in the preceding row, bring the needle out a little above the lower pink line.

10. Insert the needle below the line, and draw it through above the line for beginning the next row.

11. Make two rows, between this row and the end of the tear.

12. Beginning the fifth row above the lower line, put the needle, at the third stitch, down through the blue line or tear (Fig. 69, *c*).

13. Take two more stitches, bringing the needle out below the upper pink line.

14. Finish the row; and continue in the same manner, always putting the needle at the third stitch, *down through the tear*, to secure the edges.

15. In finishing the darn, make four rows beyond the tear.

Straightway-tear.—Darned with slanting stitches.

1. Crease, and run a square of cloth as before (Fig. 68).

2. Threading the needle with red thread, insert it at the right of the lower pink line (Fig. 70, *a*).

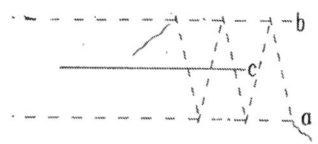

Fig. 70.—Showing the tear partly darned with slanting stitches.

CLOTH DARNING.   95

3. On a line, slanting so as to cut off one-eighth of an inch on the opposite line, take six running stitches, bringing the needle out a little below the upper line (Fig. 70, *b*), and leaving an end of the thread to be cut of later.

4. Insert the needle above the line, and pointing it towards you, take six stitches on a line, all having the same slant. Bring the needle out above the lower line at the sixth stitch.

5. Insert the needle below the lower line and take six stitches, having the same slant as before; at the fourth stitch, draw the needle down through the tear (Fig. 70, *c*).

6. Continue in this manner, always drawing the needle down through the tear, at the fourth stitch.

7. In finishing the darn, make several rows beyond the tear.

BIAS–DARN.

Materials. — Same as for a straightway-darn (page 93).

Bias-darn, or across both the warp and the woof. — A blue thread represents the tear.

1. Crease the square of cloth diagonally from corner to corner.

2. Leaving two inches at each end, run on the crease with blue thread.

3. Make two creases, one, one-fourth of an inch above; and one, one-fourth of an inch below the running.

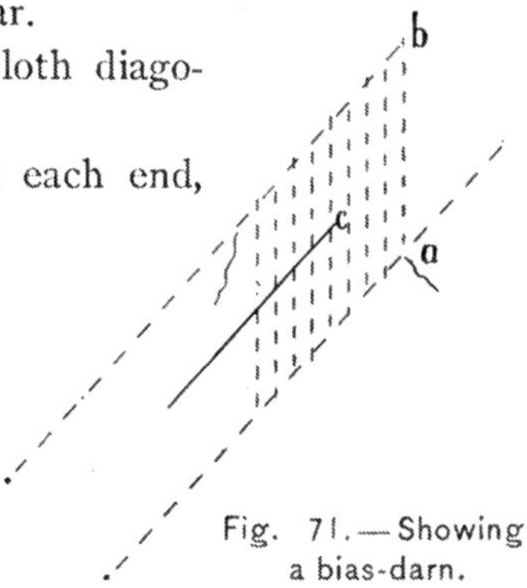

4. Leaving an inch and a fourth at both ends, make a running on each crease with pink thread.

Fig. 71. — Showing a bias-darn.

5. Thread the needle with red thread.

6. At the right, and beyond the blue line or tear, make four rows of eight stitches each, (as for a straightway-darn, page 94) *on a line with the vertical threads of the cloth* (Fig. 71).

7. Beginning the fifth row above the lower line, draw the needle down through the tear at the fourth stitch (Fig. 71, *c*).

8. Take three more stitches, bringing the needle out below the upper line.

9. Insert the needle above the line, to finish the row; drawing it out below the line for the next row.

10. Continue in this manner, always drawing the needle down through the tear, at the fourth stitch.

11. In finishing the darn, make several rows beyond the tear.

Corner–Darn.

Materials.— Same as for a straightway-darn (page 93).

Corner-darn.— A blue thread represents the tear.

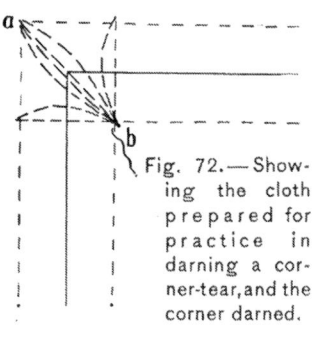

Fig. 72.— Showing the cloth prepared for practice in darning a corner-tear, and the corner darned.

1. Crease one side of the cloth one inch from the edge.

2. At right angles with the crease, make another crease one inch from the edge.

3. Call the vertex of the angle *a* (Fig. 72).

4. With the pink thread run on the crease, on both sides of the angle, one and a half inches from point *a* (Fig. 72).

5. Crease an angle half-an-inch inside the first angle.

6. With the pink thread, run on the crease, on both sides of the angle, one inch (Fig. 72).

7. Crease half-way between the two angles, and run with blue thread.

8. Using red thread, make a large knot (cut it off afterwards), and insert the needle from the right side, at the corner (Fig. 72, *b*). The knot is made to aid in drawing up the corner.

9. Run to point *a*, putting the needle down through the tear, at the fourth stitch.

10. Slightly curving to the right, return to point *b*.

11. Make a row very close and to the left of the first row, taking the stitches alternately.

12. Slightly curving to the left, return to point *b*.

13. At the left, make a row directly on a line with a thread of the cloth, to the outer pink line.

14. Make a curved line at the right to point *b*.

15. On the opposite side of the corner, make a row on a line with a thread of the cloth, as far as the outer pink line.

16. Making a line, curving to the left, return to point *b*.

17. Beginning at the corner, darn both sides with vertical stitches (page 94), or slanting stitches (page 94).

Darning with a Piece Underneath.

In darning a tear, where the garment is worn thin, or is badly torn and ravelled, a piece of cloth should be placed underneath.

1. Cut the piece larger than the tear, being careful to match *the grain of the cloth, also the figures and stripes.*
2. Draw the tear into place, and baste the right side of the piece to the wrong side of the garment, matching it exactly.
3. Baste around the edge of the tear.
4. Take either vertical stitches (page 94), or slanting stitches (page 94), through both thicknesses of cloth.
5. If the hole is large, darn the sides of the tear separately, tucking the ravellings under with the point of the needle, as you come to them.
6. After the darn is finished, lightly secure the piece on the wrong side, or cut it off near the darning.

Fine Drawing on Heavy Woollen Material.

1. Use very fine sewing silk, and hold the edges of the tear flat upon the left forefinger.
2. Inserting the needle half-an-inch below the edge of the tear, run it through half the thickness of cloth, concealing the silk.
3. Inserting the needle in the opposite edge, run through the cloth in the same manner.
4. Draw the edges closely together.
5. Continue in this manner, being careful not to lap the edges.
6. Brush up the nap on the right side.
7. Dampen, and press on the wrong side with a hot iron.

It is better to do the darning on the wrong side; but, if the garment is lined, it may be done on the right side, being careful to insert the needle in the cloth exactly where it came out.

Another way to darn a tear on heavy material is to overcast the raw edges closely together, on the wrong side, then rub the seam open and darn lightly. Lay a wet cloth over the darn, and press.

To make a perfectly flat seam on selvedges or heavy woollen cloth, the edges may be joined, as in Fig. 73.

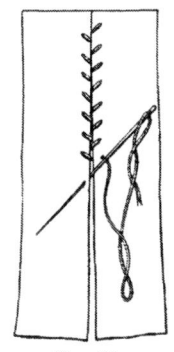

Fig. 73.

Suggestions. — The aim in darning a tear is to repair the rent so nicely that it can not be perceived. In darning twilled material, instead of taking the stitches alternately, make them in slanting rows to correspond with the twill. A rent should be repaired with fine thread or silk, matching the material in quality and color ; if the same color can not be obtained, use lengthwise ravellings of the material. On fine woollen goods, hair can be used, and the needle should be threaded with the root. When darning with very fine thread or ravellings, use short needlefuls. As fine a needle as possible should be used.

Darning can be done on the right or wrong side, according to the material. For a tear in coarse material, the stitches should be taken more than one-fourth of an inch from the edge. The closeness of the rows of stitches depends upon the material and the tear. Edges should always be worked *in and out alternately* to secure them. Always protect the ends of a tear by darning beyond them. To keep the edges of a long tear even, it is best to begin to darn in the middle. When a darn is finished, it should be dampened and pressed on the wrong side, or a thin, damp cloth can be laid on the right side and pressed. To mend a rip in the seam of a kid-glove, overhand the edges together on the right side, using fine thread or sewing silk matching the color of the glove. If there is a strain coming on the seam, button-hole stitch the edges, and then overhand the purls of the stitches together.

> For what is cloth darning used? How should the tear be held? Where should the needle be inserted? What kind of stitches should be taken? What threads are taken up in the second row? Where should the needle be put at the third stitch in the fifth and succeeding rows? How should the stitches on a bias-darn be taken? Where should the needle be inserted in a corner-darn? Why is a knot made? How many rows of stitches are made at the corner? What is the aim in darning? What can be used instead of thread? What should be done after a darn is finished? How should a kid-glove be mended?

PATCHING.

A patch is a piece of cloth, sewed on to a garment to repair it.

Hemming on a Patch.

Materials. — No. 9 needle, No. 80 thread, scissors, pins, and a piece of cotton cloth, five inches square; for the patch, a piece of cloth four inches square.

Hemming on a patch. — 1. Crease the garment, represented by the large piece of cloth, through, and across the centre (Fig. 74).

2. Mark the centre by a pin-hole, and half-an-inch from the centre on each crease, make a pin-hole.

3. Crease a square on a line with the holes, and by a thread (Fig. 74, *a*, *b*, *c*, and *d*).

4. Cut out the square on the creasing, being careful about the corners.

PATCHING.

5. Cut diagonally one-fourth of an inch at each corner (Fig. 74, *1, 2, 3,* and *4*).

6. Fold and crease each edge of the hole, by a thread, and baste.

7. Cut off each corner of the patch one-fourth of an inch deep.

Fig. 74.— Showing the large piece of cloth with the dotted lines representing where it is creased, and the plain lines where it should be cut.

8. Holding the right side of the patch towards you, fold towards you, and crease, by a thread, one-fourth of an inch deep, on all four sides.

9. Crease through, and across the centre of the patch.

10. Place the garment on the desk, with the *wrong side* upwards.

11. Place the folded edges of the patch upon the garment, *with the warp of the two pieces parallel.*

12. Match the creases, and put in pins.

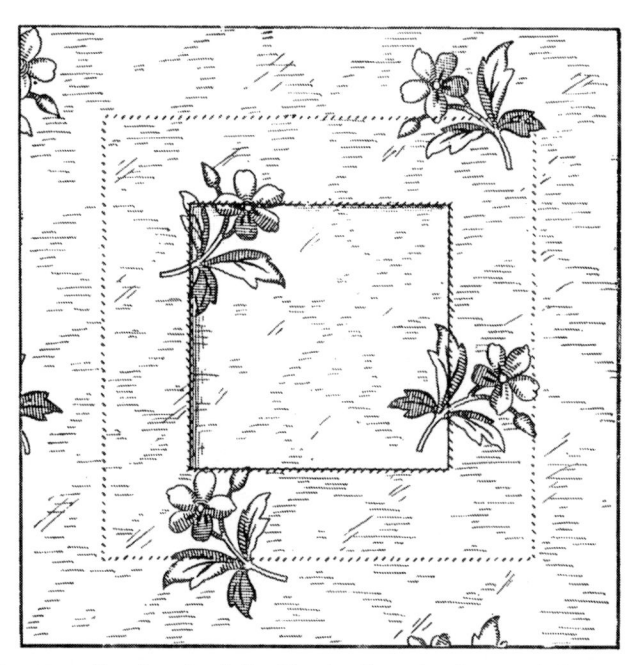

Fig. 75. — Showing the right side of a figured-calico patch, hemmed.

13. With each edge of the patch even with a thread of the garment, baste ; turning the corners neatly, by tucking the extra fold underneath with the point of the needle.

14. Turn the other side towards you, and pin the edges of the hole down at each corner.

15. Baste, keeping each edge on a thread of the patch.

PATCHING. 103

16. Hem the garment to the patch, being careful to firmly sew the corners, keeping them at right angles.

17. On the other side, hem the patch to the garment, allowing the stitches to appear as little as possible on the right side.

Fig. 76. — Showing the right side of a figured-calico patch, overhanded.

18. Take out the basting threads, and press on the wrong side.

OVERHANDING ON A PATCH.

Materials. — Same as before, with the cloth for the patch three inches square.

Overhanding on a patch. — 1. Crease the garment, represented by the large piece of cloth, through, and across the centre (Fig. 74).

2. Cut a *small* piece out of the centre, to aid later in cutting the hole.

3. Cut across each corner of the patch one-fourth of an inch deep.

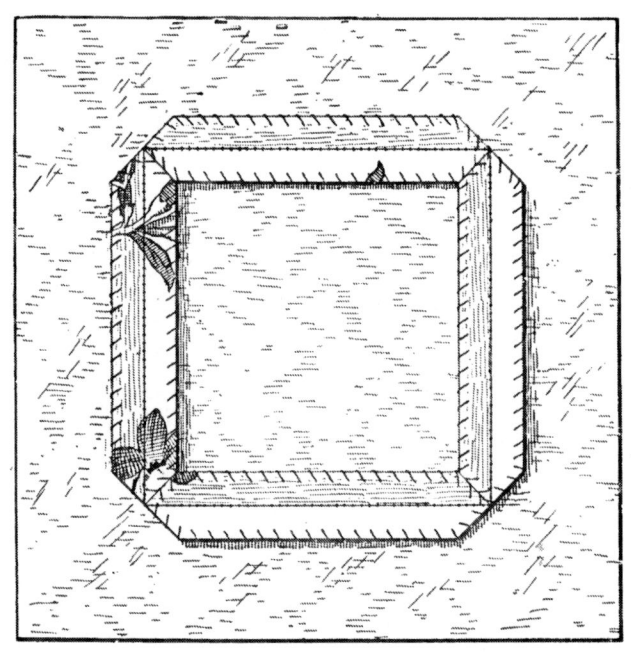

Fig. 77. — Showing the wrong side of a figured-calico patch, overhanded.

4. Holding the wrong side of the patch towards you, make a crease, by a thread, one-fourth of an inch deep, on the four sides.

5. Crease through, and across the centre of the patch.

6. Place the garment on the desk, with the right side upwards.

PATCHING.

7. Place the folded edges of the patch upon the garment, *with the warp of the two pieces parallel.*

8. Match the creases, and put in pins.

9. With the edges of the patch even with the threads of the garment, baste; turning the corners neatly, by tucking in the extra fold underneath.

10. Holding the patch towards you, fold and crease the garment even with one edge of the patch.

11. Holding the two edges securely, overhand them, sewing the corners firmly.

12. Fold and overhand the next side in the same manner, and so continue, till all the sides are overhanded (Fig. 76).

13. Take out the basting threads.

14. Turn the wrong side towards you, and carefully cut a hole in the garment, one-fourth of an inch inside the overhanding stitches.

15. At each corner, cut diagonally *to the overhanding stitches.*

16. Open the seam and overcast all the edges (Fig. 77), or work them with the blanket-stitch.

17. Dampen the seams, and press on the wrong side.

CATCH-STITCHING ON A FLANNEL PATCH.

Materials. — No. 9 needle, fine silk to match the flannel, pins, and a piece of flannel five inches square; for the patch, a piece of flannel three inches and a half square.

Catch-stitching on a patch. — 1. Crease the garment, represented by the large piece of flannel, through, and across the centre (Fig. 74).

2. Mark the centre by inserting a pin; and one inch from the middle of each crease, insert a pin.

106   SCHOOL NEEDLEWORK.

3. Crease a square, by a thread, on a line with the pins.

4. Cut the square out on the creasing, being careful in cutting the corners.

5. Crease through, and across the centre of the patch.

6. Place the garment on the desk, with the wrong side upwards.

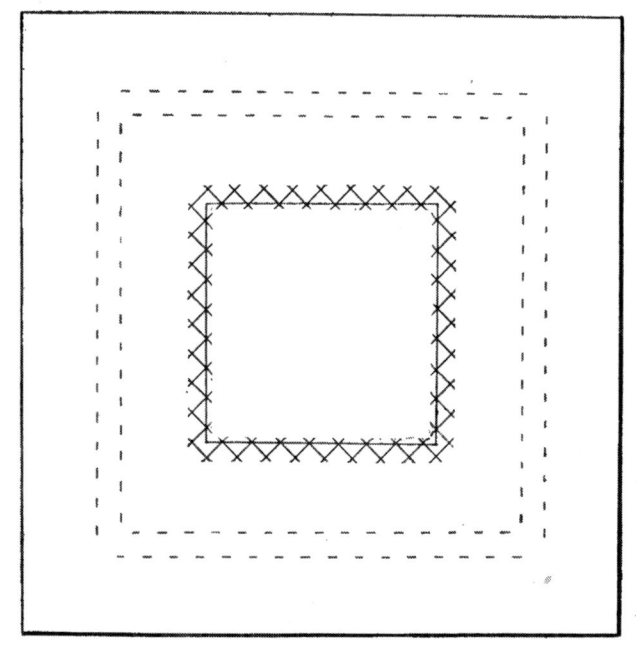

Fig. 78. — Showing the right side of the patch; the straight lines represent the edges of the hole.

7. Place the right side of the patch upon the garment, *with the nap of the two pieces running the same way.*

8. Match the creases, and put in pins.

9. With each edge of the patch even with a thread of the garment, baste one-fourth of an inch from the edge.

PATCHING. 107

10. Holding the garment towards you, baste one-fourth of an inch from the edge of the hole.

11. Draw the needle through the garment from underneath, one-eighth of an inch from the raw edge.

12. Catch-stitch (see page 117) around the square, taking the inner stitches through the patch, close to the edge of

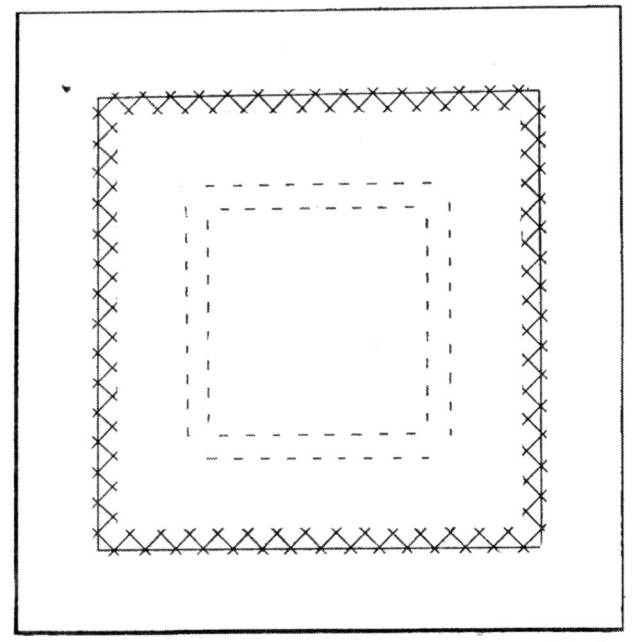

Fig. 79.— Showing the wrong side of the patch; the straight lines represent the edges of the patch.

the garment; and the outside stitches one-eighth of an inch from the edge, and through both thicknesses of cloth (Fig. 78).

13. Turning the wrong side towards you, catch-stitch in the same manner, the edges of the patch to the garment (Fig. 79).

14. Take out the basting threads, and press on the wrong side.

Suggestions. — In practical mending, judgment and consideration are necessary, and the material should be treated as common sense suggests; the object is to replace the torn or worn part with as little display as possible.

A patch can be put on in various ways: as, hemming on the right side and overcasting the raw edges together on the wrong side; it can also be put on by stitching. A patch can be overhanded on the wrong side, so that the stitches may show less, but the corners are not easily turned. Catch-stitching should be used, when the material does not easily ravel, as on flannel. Thin, woollen materials can be hemmed. When a material is worn, it is better to hem the patch on, for, if it is overhanded, the strain comes on one thread at each side.

Stripes, checks and figures should *always match*, as otherwise they attract attention. Care must be taken to have the warp and the woof of the patch run the same way as those of the garment, the straightest threads of the cloth generally represent the warp. The nap must also run in the same direction, which can be ascertained by passing the hand lightly over it. A patch can be either square or oblong, according to the shape of the damaged part, but should be large enough to cover the worn place. Fine thread or silk, matching the material, should be used; silk should be chosen a shade darker than the material, as it will work lighter.

What is a patch? What is its use? In hemming on a patch, on which side of the garment should the patch be placed? On which side, in overhanding on a patch? How should the wrong side of an overhanded patch be finished? What stitch is used in patching flannel? Which side of the garment is the patch placed upon? What is the object of patching? What care should be taken concerning the warp and the woof?

BIAS PIECING.

Bias piecing is the joining of two diagonal edges of cloth.

Materials. — No. 8 needle, No. 60 thread, pins, scissors, and a piece of calico five inches square, cut by a thread.

Fig. 80. — Showing the strips placed in a line before joining.

Bias piecing. — 1. Fold the square diagonally, from corner to corner.

2. Crease the fold, and cut on the crease.

3. From each piece of calico, cut two bias strips, each being one inch wide.

4. With the right sides upwards, place the strips on the desk in a line for joining, as in Fig. 80.

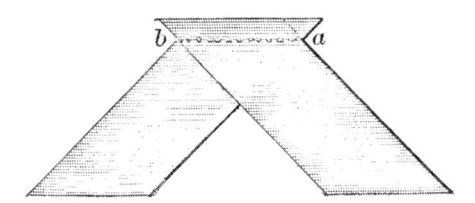

Fig. 81. — Showing the two edges sewed.

5. Place the right sides of the two middle pieces together, with the edges of the ends that are to meet even.

6 Move the edge of the upper piece, one-fourth of an inch to the left (Fig. 81).

7. Holding the edges securely, insert the needle at *a* (Fig. 81) and sew across to *b* (Fig. 81), with a running and a backstitch.

8. Press open the seam, and cut off the corners that protrude.

9. Join the other two pieces in a similar manner, except that the upper edge must be moved *to the right*.

Suggestions. — To join the ends evenly, the seam must be begun at the vertex of one of the angles, formed at the side by the two pieces of cloth, and finished at the other. When many bias strips are required, they can be easily and accurately cut, by measuring for four widths, and then cutting into halves and quarters.

<small>What is bias piecing? Where should you begin so as to join the ends evenly? Where finish?</small>

PIPING.

Piping is a cord covered with material cut on the bias, and is used to strengthen and finish the edge of a garment.

Materials. — No. 8 needle, No. 60 thread, a small cord eleven and a half inches long, a bias strip of cotton cloth twelve inches long and one inch wide and a piece of cotton cloth eleven and a half inches long, four inches wide, hemmed at the ends and one side.

Piping. — 1. Place the cord on the wrong side of the bias strip, one-fourth of an inch from the lengthwise edge, and one-fourth of an inch from the end.

2. Fold the end of the bias strip, and then folding the edge over, baste close to the cord.

CORNERS MITRED.

3. Holding the cord downwards, place the wrong side of the strip to the right side of the piece of cloth, with the raw edge of the fold even with the raw edge of the cloth.

4. Sew the piping to the edge, with a running and a backstitch, keeping close to the cord.

5. Turn to the wrong side, and hem the opposite edge down.

What is piping? For what is it used?

CORNERS MITRED.

To mitre a corner is to join two edges of cloth, so that they form a right angle.

To mitre Two Strips of Cloth.

Materials. — No. 8 needle, No. 60 thread, scissors, and a piece of calico five inches square, cut by a thread.

To mitre two strips of cloth. — 1. Fold and crease the square diagonally from corner to corner.

2. Cut on the crease.

3. From one of the pieces cut two bias strips, each strip being one inch wide.

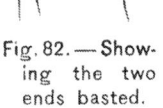

4. Place the right sides of the strips of calico together, so that the two ends are exactly even (Fig. 82).

Fig. 82. — Showing the two ends basted.

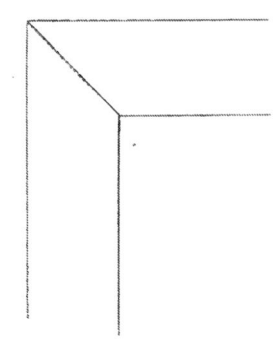

Fig. 83. — Showing the right side of a mitred corner.

112   SCHOOL NEEDLEWORK.

5. Holding the ends even, half-backstitch, by a thread, one-fourth of an inch from the edge (Fig. 82).

6. Press the seam open, and trim the corners (Fig. 83).

To mitre the Corners of a Hem.

Materials. — No. 8 needle, No. 60 thread, pins, scissors, and a piece of cotton cloth five inches square, cut by a thread.

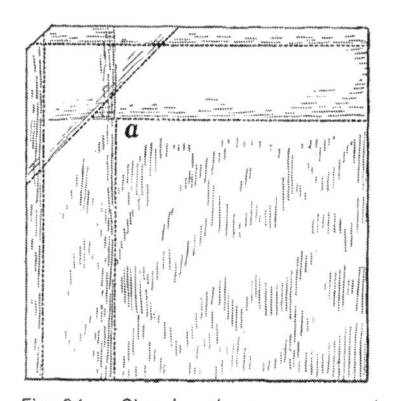

Fig. 84. — Showing the corner creased for cutting.

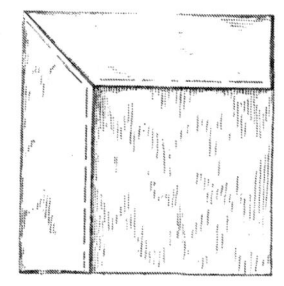

Fig. 85. — Showing the corner and hems basted.

To mitre the corner of a hem. — 1. Cut off one corner, one-fourth of an inch deep.

2. Fold, one-fourth of an inch, the two sides which are at right angles with this corner, and crease by a thread.

3. On each side make a crease, by a thread, one inch from the edge of the fold (Fig. 84), for a hem.

4. Make a pin-hole where the creases meet (Fig. 84, *a*).

5. Open all the folds, and make a diagonal crease across the corner, one-fourth of an inch outside the pin-hole (Fig. 84).

6. Cut on the crease.

7. Holding the bias edge of the cloth, at the upper left-hand side, fold and baste, by a thread, the upper hem.

8. Fold and crease the bias edge one-fourth of an inch.

9. Fold the hem at the side, making the edges of the two hems meet at a right angle (Fig. 85).

10. Baste the corner fold and side hem.

11. Hem the folds down, taking the stitches at the corner fold through only one thickness of cloth.

What is mitreing a corner? How are the strips placed together? How should the edges of the two hems meet?

LOOPS OF TAPE.

Fold the middle of the tape so as to form a point, as in Fig. 86. Overhand the inner edges for three-fourths of an inch, beginning at the ends. Fold the ends under, one-fourth of an inch, and place them on the wrong side of the cloth, one-half an inch from the edge. Baste and hem them down on three sides. Turn to the right side, and stitch the edge of the cloth to the loop.

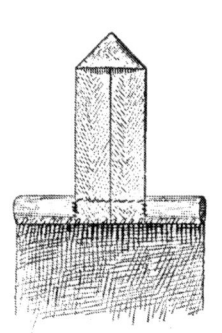

Fig. 86.— Showing a loop of tape.

PART III.

ORNAMENTAL STITCHES.

HEM-STITCH.

Hem-stitching is a method of hemming, in which the threads of the cloth are drawn and separated.

Materials. — No. 8 needle, No. 50 thread, and a lengthwise strip of linen crash.

Hem-stitch, from right to left. — 1. One inch from a lengthwise edge of the cloth, draw out from four to six threads (see suggestions) according to the coarseness of the cloth.

2. Carefully baste the hem to the line thus drawn.

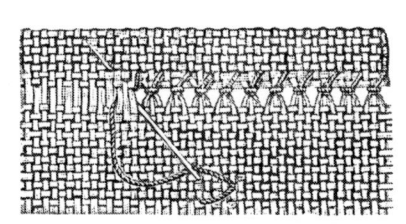

Fig. 87. — Showing hem-stitching done from right to left, needle in position.

3. Begin at the right-hand side, as for hemming.

4. Pointing the needle towards you, take up three or four cross-threads, and draw the thread through.

5. Put the needle back, take up the same threads, and insert the needle exactly above in the fold of the hem (Fig. 87).

6. Continue in the same manner, drawing the thread tight, to separate the cross-threads.

Hem-stitch, from left to right. — 1. Draw the threads, and baste the hem as before.

2. Fasten the thread in the hem, at the left-hand side.

3. Pointing the needle towards you, take up three or four cross-threads.

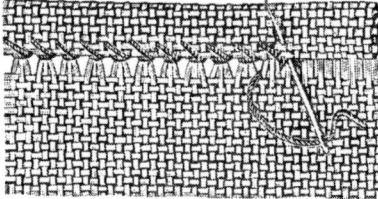

Fig. 88. — Showing hem-stitching done from left to right, needle in position.

4. Draw the needle through, and insert it in the fold of the hem exactly above where it was inserted under the cross-threads (Fig. 88).

5. Continue in the same manner, drawing the thread tight.

Suggestions. — To draw the threads, choose a coarse thread, one-fourth of an inch from the edge, and pick it out with the point of the needle. Holding this end with the right hand, draw it out carefully, continually pushing the gathers towards the opposite end with the left hand. Should the thread break, hold the cloth to the light, and again pick out the end of the thread. The chief difficulty is in drawing the first thread. Threads can be drawn any width desired.

Hem-stitching can be done either lengthwise or crosswise of the cloth. On fine materials, do not count the threads, as it is too great a strain on the eyes, and for this reason, school-girls should not do much drawn-work.

CATCH OR HERRINGBONE-STITCH.

Catch-stitch is a kind of cross-stitch, used to secure the edges of flannel.

Materials. — A long-eyed needle, a knot of split zephyr, and a piece of canvas.

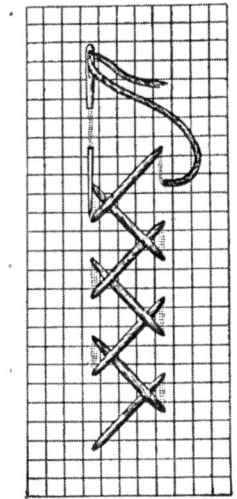

Fig. 89. — Showing catch-stitches, and the needle in position; the straight lines represent the threads of the canvas.

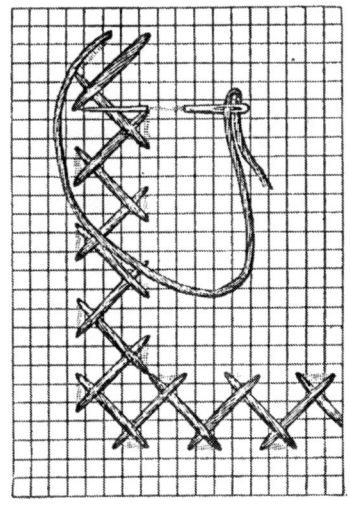

Fig. 90. — Showing a corner turned, and the needle in position for turning a corner.

Catch-stitch. — 1. Work from you, holding the canvas over the left forefinger.

2. Insert the needle from underneath, at the lower left-hand corner.

3. From the place where the zephyr comes out, count to the right four threads, then forward four threads;

insert the needle, and pointing it towards you take up two threads.

4. From the place where the zephyr comes out, count to the left four threads, then forward four threads, and take up two threads as before.

5. Continue in the same manner, making the stitches to the right, then to the left; the zephyr crossing diagonally (Fig. 89).

6. Notice that the little cross at one side, comes between the crosses on the opposite side, and that the needle comes out on a line with its insertion for the previous stitch.

7. Turn the corner, by taking a stitch at the left, insert the needle at the right, and pointing it towards the left, take up two threads (Fig. 90). Turn the canvas, and holding the next side across the left forefinger, continue as before (Fig. 90).

Suggestions. — In catch-stitching on flannel, small knots may be made if they can be concealed. When ending, fasten the thread by running it in and out under the last stitch. The thread can be fastened in beginning and finishing, by leaving an end to be sewed over and over with fine cotton on the wrong side.

The raw edge of a hem on woollen material may be fastened by catch-stitches, to avoid the ridge formed by folding the edge. The edges of a seam in flannel may be fastened in several ways; the seam may be folded to one side, and the edges fastened by a row of catch-stitches; the seam may be opened and each edge fastened separately; or, with the seam opened, a row of catch-stitches may be put in the middle.

FEATHER-STITCH.

Feather-stitching is used for ornamenting garments, etc.

Materials. — A long-eyed needle, a knot of split zephyr, and a piece of canvas.

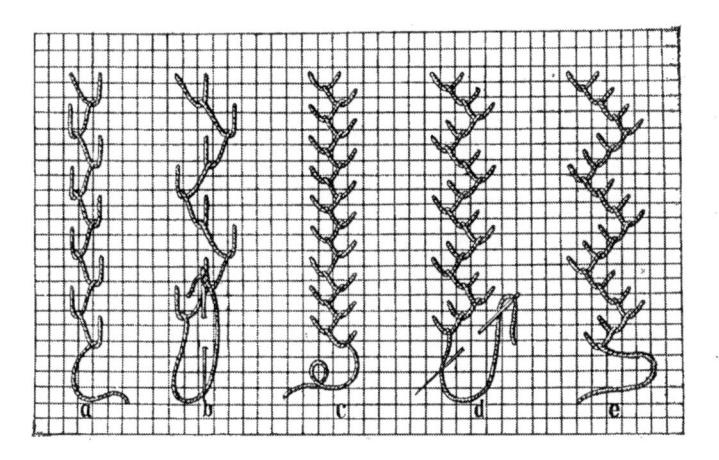

Fig. 91. — *a*, Showing single feather-stitches, taken on a line with the threads of the cloth; *b*, showing double feather-stitches, taken on a line with the threads of the cloth; *c*, showing single feather-stitches, taken slanting across the threads of the cloth; *d*, showing double feather-stitches, taken slanting across the threads of the cloth; *e*, showing treble feather-stitches, taken slanting across the threads of the cloth.

Feather-stitch. — 1. Work towards you, holding the canvas over the left forefinger.

2. Draw the needle through from underneath at the upper left-hand corner (Fig. 91, *b*).

3. From the place where the zephyr comes out, count two threads to the right, insert the needle, and pointing it towards you take up two threads of the canvas.

4. Draw the needle out over the zephyr, which is held down by the thumb.

5. From the place where the zephyr comes out, count two threads to the right, and take a stitch as before.

6. From the place where the zephyr comes out, count two threads to the left, and take a stitch, being careful to hold the zephyr down with the thumb.

7. From the place where the zephyr comes out, count two threads to the left, and take another stitch.

8. Continue taking the stitches in this way (Fig. 91, *b*).

Suggestions. — For fastening the thread see catch-stitching (page 118). This stitch may be changed into various designs, as in Fig. 91. Whatever the pattern, the stitches should be compact and uniform.

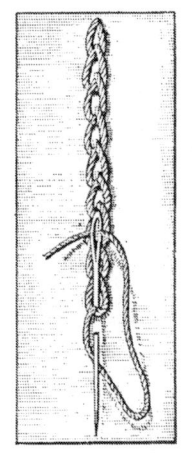

Fig. 92. — Showing chain-stitches, needle in position.

CHAIN-STITCH.

Chain-stitching is a method of embroidering, by which the stitches resemble a chain.

Materials. — An embroidery needle, embroidery silk, and a strip of cloth.

Chain-stitch. — 1. Work towards you, holding the cloth over the left forefinger.

2. Draw the needle through from underneath at the upper end, a short distance from the edge.

3. Holding the thread to the left with the thumb, insert the needle where the thread comes out, and bring it

through one-eighth of an inch below, and over the thread to form the loop.

4. Continue in this manner, always inserting the needle inside the loop of the last stitch, and being careful to take the same number of threads on the needle for each stitch.

Suggestion. — Chain-stitching is often used for outlining a pattern.

KENSINGTON OUTLINE-STITCH.

Kensington outline-stitching is done by taking a long stitch forward on the upper side, and a short stitch backward on the under-side of the cloth, and is used to form a line for ornament.

Materials.—An embroidery needle, embroidery silk, and a strip of cloth.

Kensington outline-stitch.—1. Work from you, holding the cloth over the left forefinger.

2. Draw the needle through from underneath, at the lower end.

3. Insert the needle one-eighth of an inch above, and two or three threads to the right, bringing it out at the left one-sixteenth of an inch above the place where the thread comes through the cloth (Fig. 93).

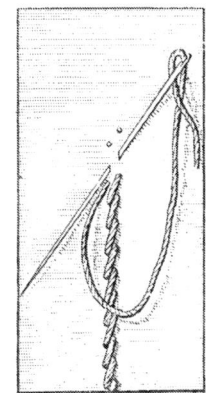

Fig. 93. — Showing Kensington outline-stitches, needle in position.

4. Continue in this way, keeping the thread to the right of the needle, and being careful not to draw the stitches tight.

Suggestions. — Some prefer keeping the thread to the left of the needle. Stem-stitching is similar to outline-stitching, except that the needle is put farther back.

BLANKET-STITCH.

Blanket-stitching is used to secure and ornament the edges of woollen material.

Materials. — An embroidery needle, embroidery silk, and a strip of flannel.

Blanket-stitch. — 1. Work from left to right, holding the edge of the flannel towards you.

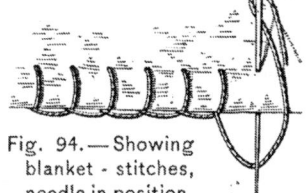

Fig. 94. — Showing blanket-stitches, needle in position.

2. Beginning at the corner, insert the needle one-fourth of an inch from each edge, and take two running stitches to the edge, leaving an end of the thread to be cut off afterwards. This brings the thread in position for working.

3. Holding the thread under the left thumb, put the needle in where it was first inserted.

4. Draw the needle through and over the thread (Fig. 94).

5. Holding the thread down with the thumb, insert the needle one-fourth of an inch to the right, and parallel with the previous stitch.

6. Draw the needle through, and over the thread, being careful that the thread lies loosely on the edge of the flannel.

BLANKET-STITCH.   123

7. Continue in this manner.

8. To fasten the thread, turn to the wrong side, take a running stitch under the last blanket-stitch. Draw the thread through, and cut it off.

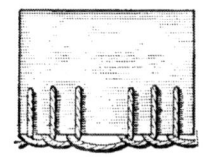

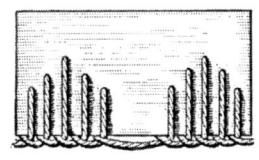

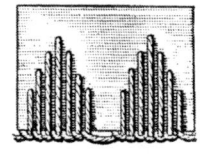

Fig. 95.—Showing blanket-stitches taken in different forms.

9. To join the thread, put the needle in under the last stitch, as in beginning the work, and draw it out over the thread that lies along the edge.

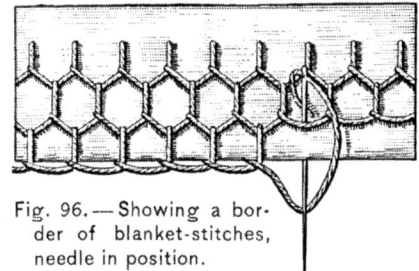

Suggestions.— If the thread is not fastened and joined carefully, the symmetry of the stitches will be broken. The order of the stitches may be varied by taking them at different depths, and leaving spaces between, as in Fig. 95.

Fig. 96.— Showing a border of blanket-stitches, needle in position.

A pretty border can be made with this stitch (Fig. 96), by making the first row the desired width from the edge, and taking the stitches for the second row through those of the first row, and so on.

EMBROIDERY KNOTS.

Embroidery knots are used for ornamentation.

Materials.— An embroidery needle, embroidery silk, and a piece of flannel.

Embroidery knot No. 1.— 1. Holding the flannel over the left forefinger, draw the needle through from underneath, at the place desired for the knot.

2. Take a *small* backstitch leaving the needle half-way through the flannel.

3. Take the silk, where it comes through the flannel, and wind it twice around the needle (Fig. 97).

4. Holding the coil under the left thumb, draw the needle through and insert it where it came through the flannel, bringing it out where the next knot is to be made.

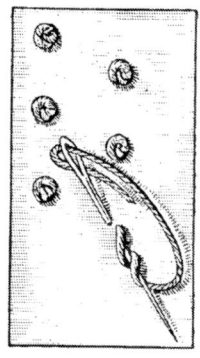

Fig. 97.— Showing embroidery knot No. 1, and the needle in position.

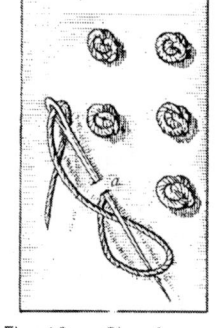

Fig. 98.— Showing embroidery knot No. 2, and the needle in position.

Embroidery knot No. 2.— 1. Holding the flannel over the left forefinger, draw the needle through from underneath, at the place desired for the knot.

2. Draw the silk towards you to the left; holding it under the thumb, bring the silk to the right, and cross below where the silk came out of the flannel (Fig. 98, *a*). Hold the loop thus formed under the thumb.

3. Insert the needle one or two threads back of *a*, bring it out at *a*, and pass it through the loop (Fig. 98).

4. Draw the needle and silk out straight upwards.

5. Insert the needle again at *a*, and bring it out where the next knot is to be made.

MARKING.

Page 126 consists of capital letters ; page 127 consists of small letters and upright numerals ; page 128 consists of small letters, suitable for fine material, and slanting numerals.

The material, thread and needle should correspond. The marking stitch consists of a cross-stitch taken over two threads of the canvas. To make the stitch, draw the needle through from underneath at the *lower right*-hand corner of the square for the stitch ; insert the needle at the *upper left*-hand corner, bringing it out at the *lower left*-hand corner ; insert the needle at the *upper right*-hand corner, and bring it out at the *lower right*-hand corner of the next stitch.

Make no knots, but leave an end of the thread to be worked over with the first stitches, or it can afterwards be run in and out under the letter. Fasten the thread in the same manner. The stitches should all be crossed the same way ; the thread should be fastened after finishing a letter, not carried from one to another. Have the back of the work look neat.

When marking on canvas is understood, fine material can be easily marked, by basting a piece of scrim over the place to be worked, and, after taking the stitches, drawing out the threads of the scrim.

126

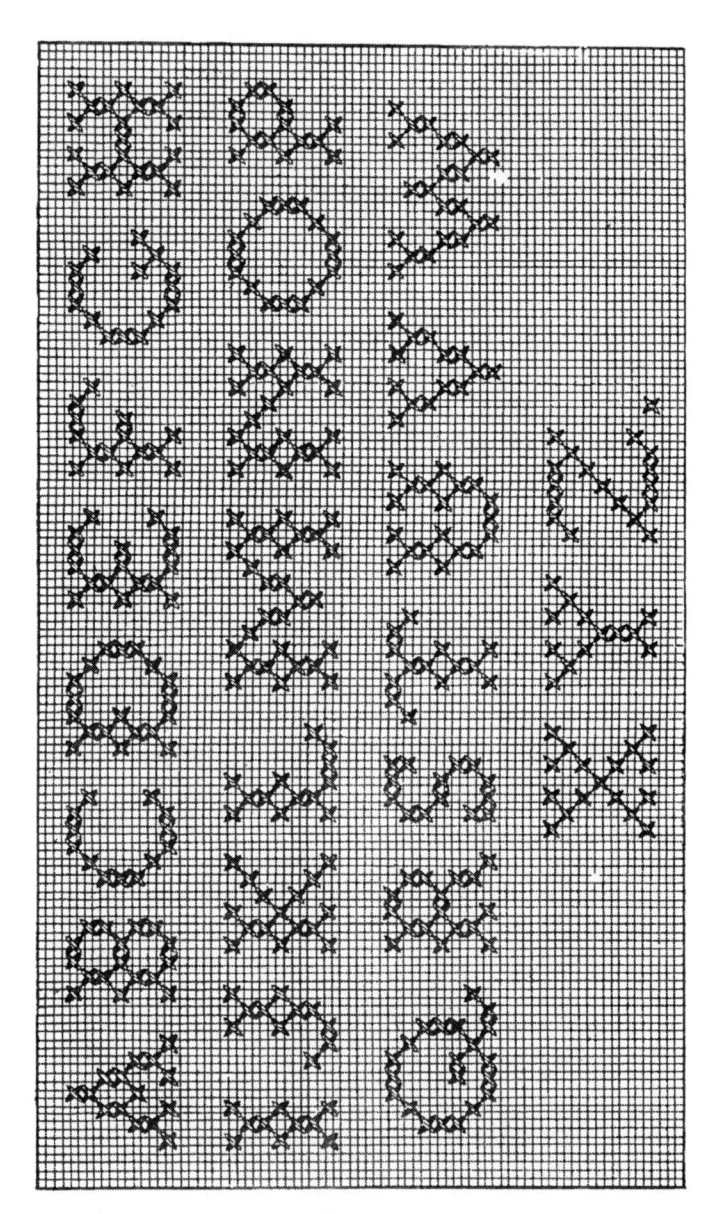

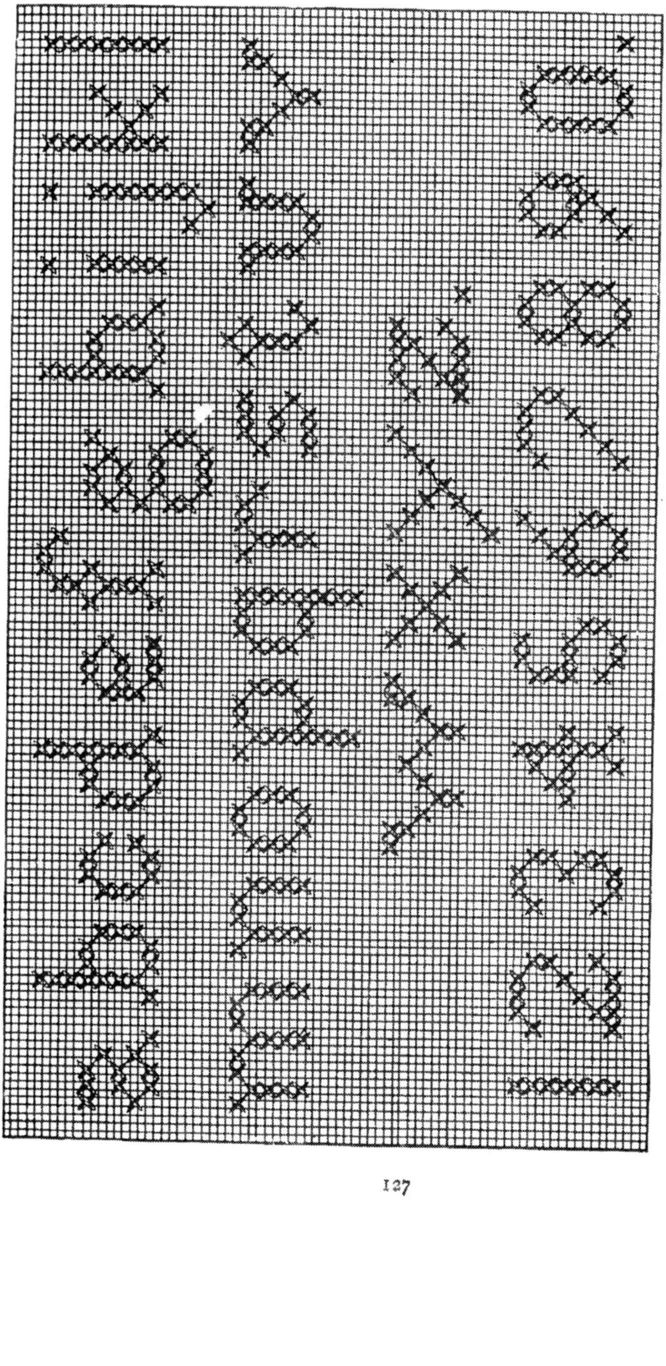

128

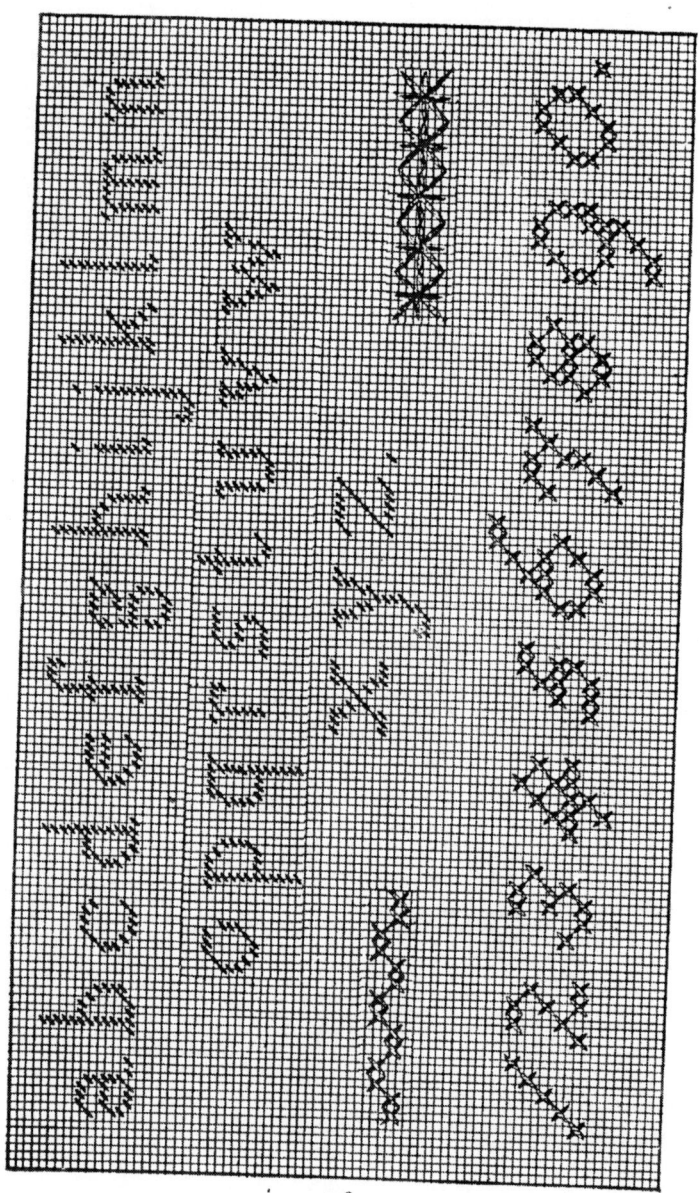

PART IV.

DRAFTING, CUTTING, AND MAKING GARMENTS.

A few general directions for the cutting of garments are here given.

A table or lap-board, large enough to lay the entire pattern upon, is required; also paper, sharp shears, weights, pins, tape-measure, needles, and thread.

The first thing to be observed in cutting is whether the cloth has a right and a wrong side. If it has a design, consider the heavier part as the bottom; a vine should run upwards; the nap on the cloth should run downwards.

Before cutting, ascertain if there is sufficient cloth by laying the different parts of the pattern upon the cloth in such positions, that the cloth will not be unnecessarily wasted; being careful in regard to the up and down of the cloth. When there is a scarcity of material, the underneath parts of the sleeves may be pieced, hems may be faced, and the small pieces may often be used for the trimmings.

The length of the main parts of a garment (as back, front, and sleeves) should be cut parallel to the selvedge or warp of the cloth. Fig. 102 represents a wrapper placed on cloth, which is folded lengthwise through the middle; the edge of the front is placed on the selvedge, and the back on the fold of the cloth, to avoid a seam at the back of the skirt. The vertical perforations in the side-back and both portions of the sleeve are placed lengthwise of the cloth. The perforations near the edges of the patterns show the seams, where alterations should be made. The perforations near the centre of the front indicate where the darts should be taken up.

In cutting plain goods, two similar parts can be cut at once by folding either the right or the wrong sides together; the selvedges or edges of the material should first be pinned together to prevent slipping. When the cloth can not be doubled, great care must be taken not to cut similar parts (as sleeves) for the same side; this can always be avoided by laying one part upon the material, with either the right or wrong sides together.

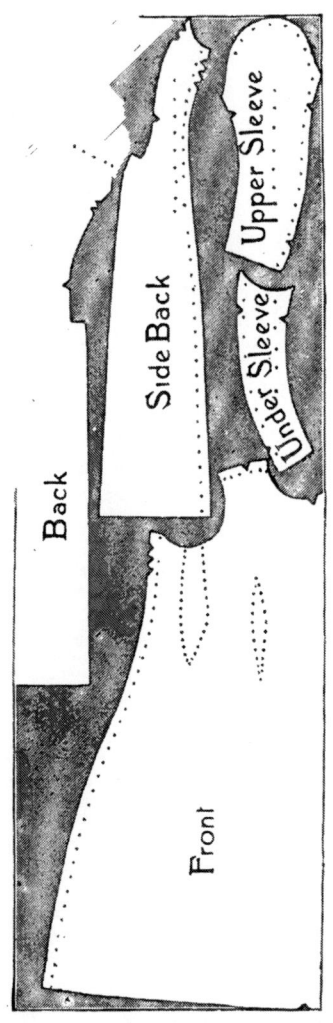

Fig. 102.— Wrapper.

Having the cloth spread

out evenly, place a weight or insert a pin at the middle of each part of the pattern. Smoothing out each part from the middle, pin it to the cloth, being careful to place pins closely at the middle of the darts, at the curves, and one at each corner of the pattern. Cut evenly and *close* to the edge of the pattern, and be very particular at the curves.

Linings should be cut and basted carefully on to the wrong side of the cloth, before cutting the cloth. The notches on the edges of the pattern should only be cut in the lining.

In cutting linings or unlined garments, the marks for the seams may be made by a tracing-wheel, or they may be pricked with a large needle. Where there are perforations, a pencil or chalk may be used. When two parts of a garment are cut at once, especially on woollen materials, the following tailor's method of marking the perforations may be used, — pin the pattern securely through both thicknesses of cloth. With a coarse, doubled thread take the first stitch in the centre of the perforation and through both thicknesses of cloth ; take another stitch in the same place, and, in drawing the thread through, leave a loop the size of a pencil. At the next perforation make a similar stitch, leaving the thread loose between the perforations, and so continue, until all the perforations are marked. Then cut out the parts, separate the two edges of cloth, as far as the thread will permit, and carefully cut the threads midway between the two edges. Cut the long stitch on the upper side, in the middle, and remove the paper pattern. The threads left in the cloth serve as a guide for basting.

Matching. — A plaided, striped, or figured cloth requires great care in cutting. If the breadths of a skirt made from a checked or evenly plaided material are cut off in the middle of a check, the breadths will readily match. In other plaids or designs, cut the lower edge of each breadth on the same line of the plaid or design. In cutting a garment, similar to a dress-waist, which opens in front, first decide what part of the plaid, stripe, or design will look best for the middle of the front and back. Then lay the pattern for the front on the cloth, so that the outer fold of the hem is one-eighth of an inch (or one-half of the width to be lapped) beyond the middle desired. Cut this side out, and cut the other half of the front, by laying the part already cut on the cloth, with the right sides together, and plaids or designs exactly matching. Lay the pattern for the back on the cloth, so that the back edge of the pattern is one-fourth of an inch beyond the middle desired; this allows for the seam. Cut the other half of the back as in cutting the second half of the front.

In order to cut twilled material on the bias, with the twill perpendicular, the cloth must be folded at right angles to the twill. To do this, lay the cloth lengthwise on the table, with the right side downward, fold over the lower right-hand corner, and cut on the fold. Linings for broad hems or a curved edge (as a hat) should be cut on the bias (see page 11).

Cotton cloth, calico, or flannel may be torn (page 9), when a straight edge is required; linen should be cut by first drawing a thread (page 116).

Drafting. — The following rules for drafting are given as suitable in ordinary cases, but the drafter should use discretion in regard to personal taste and prevailing styles.

In the illustrations, each square represents an inch. Dots are marked by letters, lines are marked by numbers. Remember that the dot is the important mark, the letter being but a name to the dot, and may be placed in any convenient position near the dot.

TWO-BREADTH APRON.

A two-breadth apron, one yard long, having a four inch hem, requires two and one-fourth yards of material.

1. Find half of the length of the material, tear across, or fold and cut on the fold.

2. Fold the lengthwise edges of one of the pieces together.

3. One and one-half inches each side of the fold, tear the entire length, or fold again one and one-half inches from the edge of the fold and cut both thicknesses of material on the last fold. This gives a strip for the binding and the two side-breadths.

Making.—Sew the raw edges of the side-breadths to the front-breadth, thus avoiding a seam in the middle. If desired, hem the sides. Make a four inch hem at the lower edge, overhanding the ends of the hem before hemming. Gather the upper edge and put it into the band, being very careful to sew securely at the ends of the gathers, as this is where a strain comes. The fulness of the gathers depends upon the width of the material and the form of the person. Overhand the edges of the band together on each side of the gathers. If strings are desired, they should be cut before sewing the breadths together. Make a narrow hem at the sides of the strings, and a broader hem at the lower end. Gather, or lay small plaits, at the other end of the strings ; insert them in the ends of the band, and hem the band over them.

CHILD'S BIB.

Take a piece of paper fifteen inches long and eleven inches wide.

1. With the long side of the paper horizontally in front of you, write your name and school at the upper left-hand corner of the paper.

2. Fold the lengthwise edges together, so that the name shows.

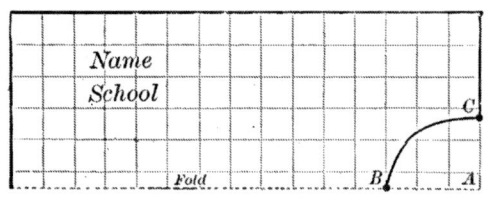

Fig. 103.—Child's Bib.

3. With the folded edge towards you, make a dot at the right-hand end of the fold ; mark it *A* (Fig. 103).

4. On the fold, make a dot three inches from *A* ; mark it *B*.

5. At the right-hand end, two and one-fourth inches above *A*, make a dot ; mark it *C*.

6. Draw a light dash-line from *B* to *C*.

7. Beyond the dash-line, draw a curved line from *B* to *C*, allowing three-fourths inch curve at the middle. Erase the dash-line.

8. Cut on the curve.

Making.—Make a narrow hem on the sides and on the straight edges at the top, and an inch hem at the lower edge. Bind the curve with narrow linen tape, leaving enough at each end for strings.

POCKETS.

Take a piece of paper fifteen inches long and six inches wide.

1. Place the narrow side of the paper horizontally in front of you.
2. Write your name and school at the lower part of the paper.
3. Make a dot six inches from the lower left-hand corner; mark it *A* (Fig. 104).
4. Make a dot one inch to the left of the upper right-hand corner; mark it *B*.
5. Make a dot four inches exactly below *B*; mark it *C*.
6. Draw from *A* to *C*.
7. Draw from *B* to *C*.
8. Cut on the outer lines.

Making.—When the skirt is made of wash material, make the pocket of the same; for woollen material, use strong silesia or cambric. Place the longest side of the pattern on a lengthwise fold of the material, and then cut. When the pocket is made of material different from the skirt, each bias edge should have a facing, two inches wide, like the material of the skirt. Baste the facings at the outside edges, and hem them at the inner edges.

Fold the edges of the pocket together, with the facings on the outside. Beginning one-fourth of an inch below *A* (Fig. 104), make a French seam at the side and across the lower edge of the pocket. On the bias edge measure six inches from the seam, and from this point, stitch to *C* (Fig. 104). Turn the pocket inside out. In a seam of the skirt, beginning four and a half inches from the binding (this distance depends upon the length of the arm), make a slit six inches long, and fasten each end securely.

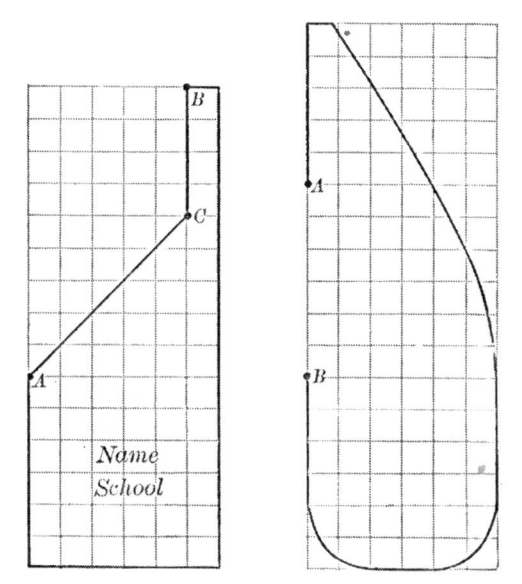

Figs. 104 and 105. — Pockets.

With the facing of the pocket to the right side of the skirt, place the lower seams exactly together; baste, and stitch the pocket in. After overcasting, turn the pocket. Fold the edges in from *B* to *C* and overhand them. Lay a small plait at the upper end of the pocket, and tack it securely to the binding.

Fig. 105 shows another way of cutting a pocket, which is to be inserted in the opening of the skirt between *A* and *B*.

CHILD'S DRAWERS.
(AGE, 8 YEARS.)

Take a piece of paper twenty-two inches long and fourteen inches wide.

1. Place the narrow side of the paper horizontally in front of you.

2. Write your name and school two inches from the left-hand side of the paper, and eight inches above the lower edge. Under the name of the school, put in a column the words, waist measure, twenty-two inches ; leg measure, seventeen inches ; knee measure, thirteen inches.

3. Mark the upper left-hand corner *A*, the upper right-hand corner *B*, the lower left-hand corner *C*, and the lower right-hand corner *D* (Fig. 106).

4. Make a dot two inches above *C* ; mark it *E*.

5. Make a dot two inches above *D* ; mark it *F*.

6. Draw a dash-line from *E* to *F*.

7. Fold the paper under on the line ; this is for the hem.

8. Make a dot seven and one-half inches above *F* ; mark it *G*.

9. Make a dot three inches below *A* ; mark it *H*.

10. Make a dot four inches to the left of *B* ; mark it *I*.

11. Draw a line from *H* to *I*.

12. Draw a line from *G* to *I*.

13. Make a dot eight and one-half inches to the right of *E* ; mark it *J*.

14. Draw a light dash-line from *G* to *J*.

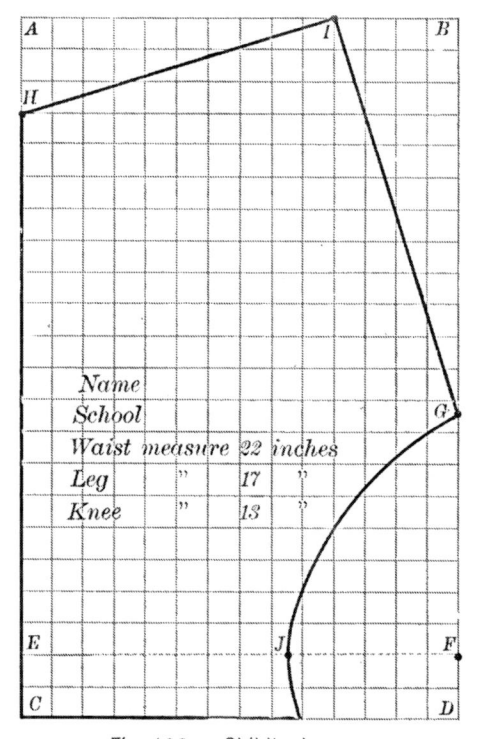

Fig. 106. — Child's drawers.

15. Draw an inward-curving line from *G* to *J*, allowing one-inch curve in the middle. Erase the dash-line.

16. Without unfolding the hem, cut the pattern on the outside lines.

Making. — For drawers this size, one and one-fourth yards of material are required. Fold the cloth lengthwise fourteen inches from one of the edges, and pin the thicknesses of cloth together at the selvedge edge. Unfold the hem, and lay the longest edge of the pattern on the fold, *with the lower edge at the raw edge of the cloth.* Carefully pin the pattern on, and then cut. Remove the pattern, lay it on the other end of the cloth in the same manner, and cut the other leg. For an opening at the side, cut a slit on each fold seven and one-half inches deep. Cut two lengthwise bindings, each three inches wide and twelve inches long. The lower edge is cut by a thread ; begin there to baste, and, if one side proves a little longer than the other, pare it off. Sew each leg as far as *G* (Fig. 106). Place the right sides of the legs together, with the seams exactly meeting. Turn one seam to the right, and the other to the left, and pin. Beginning at *G*, sew the upper portions together. Fold and sew the hem of each leg. At the side openings, make narrow hems and set in gussets. If preferred, the openings may be faced or bound. Leaving two inches at each end, gather each side, and put on the bindings, allowing more fulness at the middle.

NIGHT-DRESS YOKE.

(BUST MEASURE, 32 INCHES.)

Take a piece of paper seventeen inches long and nine inches wide.

Place the long side of the paper horizontally in front of you.

140   SCHOOL NEEDLEWORK.

Write your name and school three inches from the left-hand side of the paper, and three inches above the lower edge.

Front. — 1. Draw a vertical dash-line one and one-half inches from the left-hand side of the paper.

2. Fold the paper under on the line, this is for the hem.

3. Mark the upper left-hand corner of the paper *A*, the upper right-hand corner *B*, the lower left-hand corner *C*, the lower right-hand corner *D* (Fig. 107).

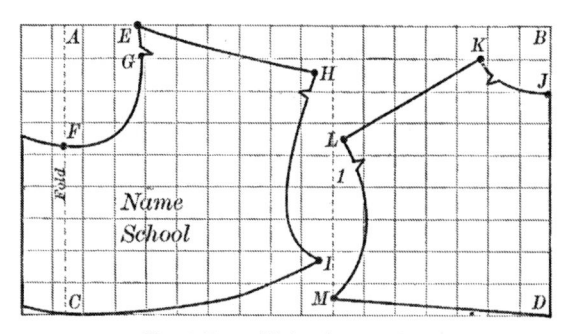

Fig. 107. — Night-dress yoke.

4. Draw a vertical dash-line eight and one-half inches from the left-hand side of the paper; mark it *I*.

5. Make a dot two and one-fourth inches to the right of *A*; mark it *E*.

6. Make a dot three and three-fourths inches below *A*; mark it *F*.

7. Make a dot one inch below *E*; one-eighth of an inch to the right of this dot make another dot; mark the last dot *G*.

8. Draw a light dash-line from *F* to *G*.

NIGHT-DRESS YOKE.

9. Draw an inward-curving line from *F* to *G*; allowing seven-eighths of an inch curve at the middle.

10. Continue the curved line to *E*. Erase the dash-line.

11. Make a dot one-half of an inch from line *I*, and one and one-fourth inches from the upper edge of the paper; mark it *H*.

12. Draw a line from *E* to *H*.

13. Make a dot one-fourth of an inch from line *I*, and one and three-fourths inches above the lower edge of the paper; mark it *I*.

14. Draw an inward-curving line, from *H* to *I*, (see shape in Fig. 107).

15. Draw a light dash-line from *C* to *I*.

16. Draw an outward-curving line, from *C* to *I*, allowing three-eighths of an inch curve at the middle. Erase the dash-line.

17. Mark a notch on the curved line, one inch from *E*.

18. Mark a notch on the curved line, one inch from *H*. The notches show where the shoulder-seam should be taken.

Back. — 1. Make a dot two inches below *B*; mark it *J*.

2. Make a dot one inch below the upper edge of the paper, and two and one-fourth inches from the right-hand edge; mark it *K*.

3. Draw a light dash-line from *J* to *K*.

4. Draw an inward-curving line from *J* to *K*, allowing three-eighths of an inch curve at the middle. Erase the dash-line.

5. Make a dot one-fourth of an inch from line *I*, and three and one-half inches below the upper edge of the paper; mark it *L*.

6. Draw a line from *K* to *L*.

7. Make a dot, on line *I*, one-half of an inch above the lower edge of the paper; mark it *M*.

8. Draw a light dash-line from *L* to *M*.

9. Draw an inward-curving line from *L* to *M*, allowing seven-eighths of an inch curve at the middle. Erase the dash-line.

10. Draw a line from *D* to *M*.

11. Mark a notch on the curved line, one inch from *L*.

12. Mark a notch on the curved line, one inch from *K*.

13. Without unfolding the hem at the front, cut the patterns on the outside lines, making the notches small.

CHILD'S SACK TIER

(Age, 2 Years.)

Take a piece of paper one yard long and twelve inches wide.

Place the narrow side of the paper horizontally in front of you. Mark the upper left-hand corner *A*, the upper right-hand corner *B*, the lower left-hand corner *C*, the lower right-hand corner *D* (Fig. 108).

Front. — 1. Make a dot twenty-one and one-half inches above *C*; mark it E.

2. Make a dot two inches above *E*; one and one-half inches to the right of this dot and parallel with it, make another dot; mark it *F*.

3. Draw a light dash-line from *E* to *F*.

4. Draw an inward-curving line from *E* to *F*, allowing three-fourths of an inch curve at the middle. Erase the dash-line.

CHILD'S SACK TIER. 143

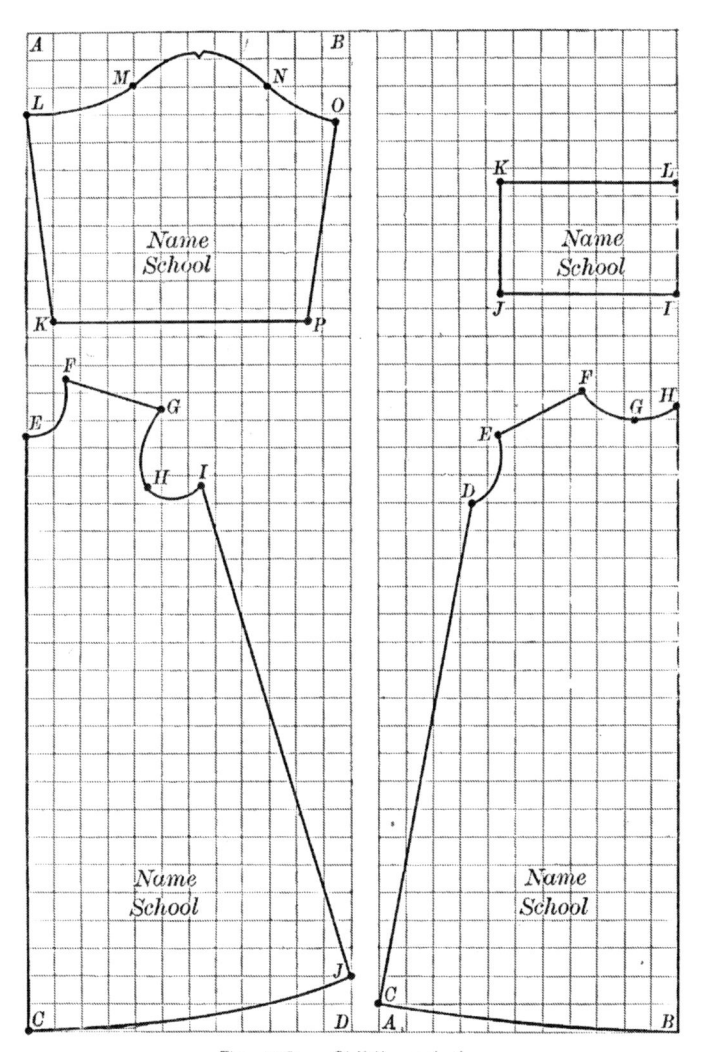

Fig. 108.—Child's sack tier.

5. Make a dot three and one-half inches to the right of *F* and parallel with *F*; one inch exactly below this dot make another dot; mark it *G*.

6. Draw a line from *F* to *G*.

7. Make a dot three inches exactly below *G*; one-half of an inch to the left of this dot make another dot; mark it *H*.

8. Draw a light dash-line from *G* to *H*.

9. Draw an inward-curving line from *G* to *H*, allowing three-eighths of an inch curve at the middle. Erase the dash-line.

10. Make a dot two inches to the right of *H*, and parallel with *H*; mark it *I*.

11. Draw an inward-curving line from *H* to *I* (see shape in Fig. 108).

12. Make a dot two inches above *D*; mark it *J*.

13. Draw a line from *I* to *J*.

14. Draw a light dash-line from *C* to *J*.

15. Draw an outward-curving line from *C* to *J*, allowing one-half of an inch curve at the middle. Erase the dash-line.

Sleeve. — 1. Make a dot ten and one-half inches below *A*; one inch to the right of this dot and parallel with it, make another dot; mark the last dot *K*.

2. Make a dot three inches below *A*; mark it *L*.

3. Draw a line from *K* to *L*.

4. Make a dot one inch above *L*; four inches to the right of this dot and parallel with it, make another dot; mark it *M*.

5. Draw a light dash-line from *L* to *M*.

6. Draw an inward-curving line from *L* to *M*, allowing three-eighths of an inch curve at the middle. Erase the dash-line.

7. Make a dot five inches to the right of *M* and parallel with *M*; mark it *N*.

8. Draw a light dash-line from *M* to *N*.

9. Draw an outward-curving line from *M* to *N*, allowing one and one-fourth inch curve at the middle. Erase the dash-line.

10. Mark a notch at the middle of this curve.

11. Make a dot two and one-half inches to the right of *N* and parallel with *N*; one and one-fourth inches exactly below this dot make another dot; mark it *O*.

12. Draw a slightly inward-curving line from *N* to *O*.

13. Make a dot nine and one-half inches to the right of *K*, and parallel with *K*; mark it *P*.

14. Draw a line from *O* to *P*.

15. Draw a line from *K* to *P*.

Take a piece of paper one yard long and eleven inches wide.

Place the narrow side of the paper horizontally in front of you. Mark the lower left-hand corner *A*; mark the lower right-hand corner *B*.

Back. — 1. Make a dot one inch above *A*; mark it *C*.

2. Draw a light dash-line from *B* to *C*.

3. Draw an outward-curving line from *B* to *C*, allowing one-fourth of an inch curve at the middle. Erase the dash-line.

4. Make a dot eighteen inches exactly above *C*; three and one-half inches to the right of this dot, and parallel with it, make another dot; mark it *D*.

5. Draw a line from *C* to *D*.

6. Make a dot one inch to the right of *D* and parallel

with D; two and one-half inches exactly above this dot make another dot; mark it E.

7. Draw an inward-curving line from D to E (see shape in Fig. 108).

8. Make a dot three inches to the right of E, and parallel with E; one and one-half inches exactly above this dot, make another dot; mark it F.

9. Draw a line from E to F.

10. Make a dot one inch exactly below F; two inches to the right of this dot, and parallel with it, make another dot; mark it G.

11. Draw a light dash-line from F to G.

12. Draw an inward-curving line from F to G, allowing three-eighths of an inch curve at the middle. Erase the dash-line.

13. Make a dot one and one-half inches to the right of G; one-fourth of an inch above this dot make another dot; mark it H.

14. Continue the curved line from G to H.

Cuff. — 1. Make a dot four inches above H; mark it I.

2. Make a dot six and one-half inches to the left of I and parallel with I; mark it J.

3. Draw a line from I to J.

4. Make a dot four inches exactly above J; mark it K.

5. Draw a line from J to K.

6. Make a dot four inches above I; mark it L.

7. Draw a line from K to L.

Write your name and school at the lower part of each pattern.

Cut each pattern out, on the heavy lines.

Making. — Lay the longest side of the front pattern on a lengthwise fold of the cloth, and cut. Fold the selvedges of the cloth together, lay the longest side of the back pattern on the selvedge edge, and cut the two backs at once. With the right sides of the cloth folded together, lay the lower edge of the sleeve pattern on a woof thread of the cloth, and cut two sleeves at once. Lay the narrow edge of the cuff pattern on a woof thread of the cloth, and cut one cuff; cut the other cuff in a similar manner. Baste an inch and a half hem at each side of the opening in the back; baste the side and shoulder-seams together, allowing half-an-inch seam. Try the tier on, make any alterations necessary, and then sew the seams. Make an inch hem at the lower edge. Sew each sleeve together, making a narrow seam. Gather the upper edge of each sleeve, leaving a space of two inches each side of the seam. Gather the lower edge of each sleeve, leaving a space of an inch and a half each side of the seam. Sew the narrow edges of each cuff together. Holding the right sides together stitch the cuffs to the sleeves. Fold the cuffs over, and hem on the wrong side at the stitching. Holding the sleeve towards you, with the upper part of the sleeve marked M (Fig. 108) towards the front, and with the notch at the shoulder-seam, sew the sleeve in. Bind or face the neck. Make the button-holes, and put on the buttons. If strings are desired make them each three inches wide and three-fourths of a yard long; laying a plait, insert the strings into the side-seams five inches below the arm-scye.

GORED SKIRT.

To make a gored skirt one yard long, having a four inch hem, three and one-third yards of material, one yard wide are required.[1] Tear off three breadths, each forty inches long.

Front-breadth. — 1. Fold the lengthwise edges of one of the breadths together.

2. Hold the folded edge towards you.

3. Make a dot at the right-hand side, ten and one-half inches above the folded edge; mark it A.

4. Make a dot four inches to the left of A and parallel with A; mark it B. This is for the hem.

5. Make a dot at the left-hand side, eight and one-half inches above the folded edge; mark it C.

6. Make a dot on the folded edge, one-half of an inch from the left-hand end; mark it D.

7. Cut straight from A to B.

8. Fold the cloth from B to C, and cut on the fold.

9. Cut from C to D, slightly curving inward.

Side-breadths. — 1. Fold the lengthwise edges of another breadth together.

2. Hold the selvedges towards you.

3. Make a dot at the right-hand side, sixteen and one-half inches from the selvedges; mark it A.

4. Make a dot four inches to the left of A, and parallel with A; mark it B.

5. Make a dot at the left-hand side, thirteen and one-half inches from the selvedges; mark it C.

6. Cut straight from A to B.

---

[1] This may be cut from paper if desired.

7. Fold the cloth from *B* to *C*, and cut on the fold.

Back-breadth. — Cut this breadth thirty (or more) inches wide.

Cut the band three and one-half inches wide, and one inch longer (to allow for lapping and making) than the waist measure.

Making. — In a gored skirt, the bias edges should be towards the back. Place the straight edges of the side-breadths to the front-breadth, and pin them together at the ends and in the middle. In sewing the seams, hold the bias edge towards you, fulling it a little if necessary; or the bias edge can be held smoothly, afterwards cutting off the extra length at the lower edge. Sew the back-breadth to the side-breadths in a similar manner. Make a four inch hem at the lower edge, laying a small plait at each seam for the fulness. In the middle of the back-breadth make a placket ten inches in length. Put the upper edge into the band, allowing more fullness at the back than in the front.

DRAWERS.

(AGE, 12 YEARS AND UPWARD.)

1. Place the narrow side of a sheet of drafting-paper horizontally in front of you.

2. Write your name and school five inches from the left-hand side of the paper and five inches above the lower edge. Under the name of the school, put in a column the words, waist measure, leg measure and knee measure.

3. Take the waist measure tightly, and record it.

4. Take the leg measure from the side of the waist to the side of the knee, and record it.

5. Take the measure around the knee, and record it.

6. Make a dot one inch from the left-hand side of the paper, and two inches above the lower edge; mark it *A* (Fig. 109).

7. From dot *A* draw an oblong (having the longest side vertical) four inches longer than the leg measure, and four inches wider than half the waist measure.

8. Mark the perpendicular line at left *1*; the upper horizontal line *2*; the perpendicular line at right *3*; the lower horizontal line *4*.

9. Make a dot on line *1*, four inches below the junction of lines *1* and *2*; mark it *B*.

10. Find half the waist measure, and make a dot on line *2* this distance from the junction of lines *1* and *2*; mark it *C*.

11. Make a dot one inch to the left of *C*; mark it *D*.

12. Make a dot two inches exactly below *D*; mark it *E*.

13. Draw a line from *B* to *C*; mark it *5*.

14. Draw a line from *B* to *E*; mark it *6*.

15. Find half the leg measure, and make a dot on line *3* this distance from the junction of lines *3* and *4*; mark it *F*.

16. Make a dot on line *4*, from *A*, two inches more than half the knee measure; mark it *G*.

17. Draw a light dash-line from *C* to *F*.

18. Draw an outward-curving line from *C* to *F*, allowing one-inch curve at the middle; mark it *7*. Erase the dash-line.

19. Draw a light dash-line from *E* to *F*.

20. Draw an inward-curving line from *E* to *F*, allowing half-an-inch curve at the middle; mark it *8*. Erase the dash-line.

DRAWERS. 151

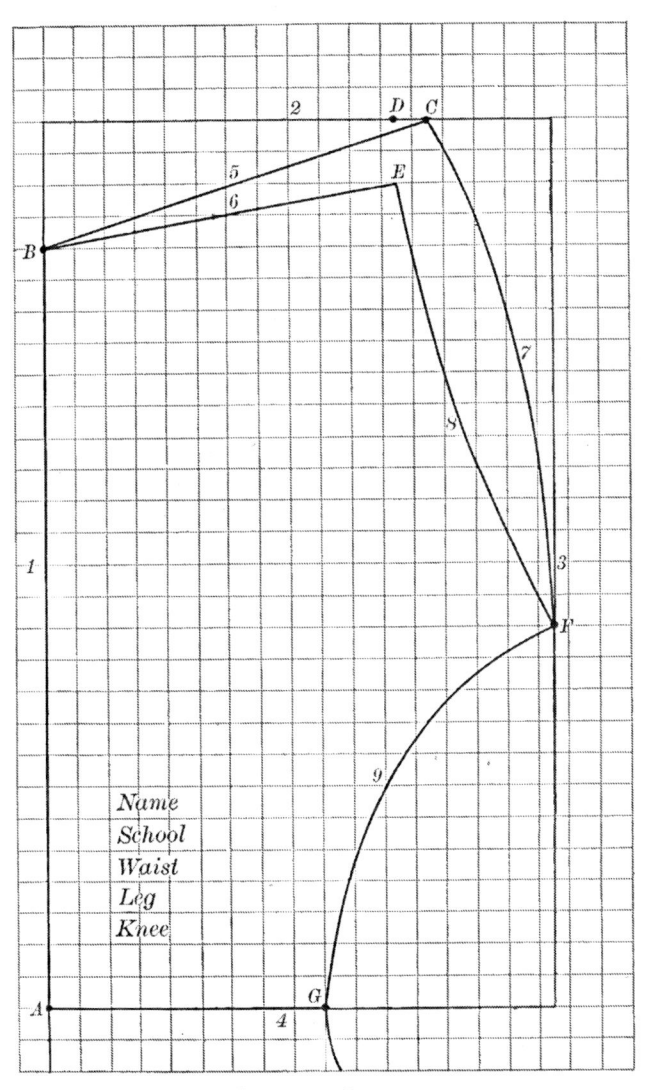

Fig. 109.—Drawers.

21. Draw a light dash-line from *F* to *G*.

22. Draw an inward-curving line from *F* to *G*, allowing a two inch curve at the middle; mark it *9*. Erase the dash-line.

23. Fold the paper under on line *4*, for the hem.

24. Without unfolding the hem, cut the pattern on the outside lines. Trace lines *6* and *8*.

Making. — Fold the cloth lengthwise, the width of the pattern from one of the edges, and pin the thicknesses of cloth together. Unfold the hem, and lay the longest side of the pattern on the fold, with the lower edge at the raw edge of the cloth. Pin the pattern on, and trace lines *6* and *8*. Cut both thicknesses of cloth at the edges of the pattern, and remove the pattern; then cut the upper fold of cloth on the traced lines, this is for the front. Cut the other leg by laying the leg already cut on the cloth, right sides together, and the lower edge on a woof thread of the cloth. Cut a binding lengthwise of the cloth, having it three inches wide and the length of the waist measure, allowing one inch for lapping at each opening. They may be made to open in the back or at the side. When tucks are to be made, allowance must be made for them before cutting the cloth. If open drawers are desired, face the upper portions of the legs; otherwise make them according to the directions on page 139. To avoid fulness at the waist, the gathers can be put into a yoke.

CHILD'S WAIST (opening in the back).

(AGE, 3 TO 10 YEARS.)

Take a piece of paper sixteen inches long and twenty inches wide.

1. Place the long side of the paper horizontally in front of you.

2. Write your name and school three inches from the left-hand side of the paper, and eight inches above the lower edge. Under the name of the school, put in a a column the words, waist measure, bust measure, length from tape to back of neck, length from tape to waist, length of shoulder.

3. Take the waist measure, and record it.

4. Take the bust measure by putting the tape-measure around the body close under the arms; pin the ends together at the middle of the chest. Record this measure, leaving the tape still in position.

5. Measure from tape to the bone in the back of the neck, and record it.

6. Measure from tape to waist, and record it.

7. Measure the length of shoulder, and record it.

8. Draw a horizontal dash-line nine inches above the lower edge of the paper; mark it *1* (Fig. 110).

9. Draw a vertical line two inches from the left-hand edge of the paper; mark it *2*.

10. Draw a vertical dash-line one inch to the right of line *2*; mark it *3*. This allows for the hem.

11. Find one-half of the bust measure, and at this distance from line *3* draw a vertical line; mark it *4*.

12. Bisect the distance between lines *3* and *4*, and half-

an-inch to the left of the middle draw a vertical dash-line; mark it *5*.

13. Draw a horizontal dash-line from line *3* to line *4*, as many inches above line *1*, as is the measure "from tape to neck"; mark it *6*.

14. Draw a horizontal dash-line from line *3* to line *4*, as far below line *1*, as the measure "from tape to waist"; mark it *7*.

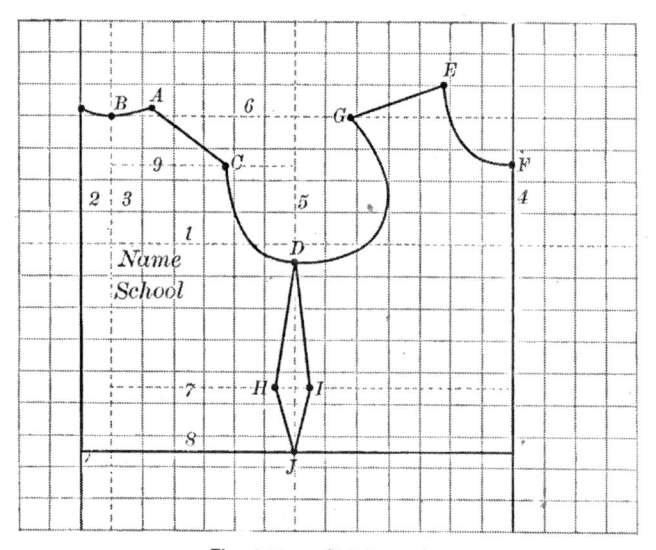

Fig. 110.—Child's waist.

15. Draw a horizontal line two inches below line *7*; mark it *8*.

BACK.

Neck.—1. Make a dot one and one-half inches to the right of line *3*, and one-fourth of an inch above line *6*; mark it *A*.

2. Make a dot at the junction of lines *3* and *6*; mark it *B*.

3. Draw a slightly curved line from *A* to *B* (see Fig. 110).

Shoulder. — 1. Draw a horizontal dash-line from line *3* to line *5*, one and one-half inches below line *6*; mark it *9*.

2. Place the end of the ruler on *A*, and, bringing the shoulder measurement to meet line *9*, make a dot; mark it *C*.

3. Draw a straight line from *A* to *C*.

Arm-scye. — 1. Make a dot half-an-inch below line *1*, on line *5*; mark it *D*.

2. Draw a curved line from *C* to *D* (see Fig. 110).

FRONT.

Neck. — 1. Make a dot two and one-fourth inches to the left of line *4*, and one inch above line *6*; mark it *E*.

2. On line *4* make a dot one and one-half inches below line *6*; mark it *F*.

3. Draw a curved line from *E* to *F* (see Fig. 110).

Shoulder. — 1. Place the end of the ruler on *E*, and, bringing the shoulder measurement to meet line *6*, make a dot; mark it *G*.

2. Draw a straight line from *E* to *G*.

Arm-scye. — To complete the arm-scye, draw a curved line from *G* to *D* (see shape in Fig. 110).

Waist. — 1. If the waist measure is less than the bust measure, divide their difference by two, and make a dot this distance on line *7* at each side of line *5*; mark them *H* and *I*.

2. Draw a straight line from *D* to *H*, and another from *D* to *I*.

3. Make a dot at the junction of lines *5* and *8*; mark it *J*.

4. Draw a straight line from *H* to *J*, and another from *I* to *J*.

If the waist measure is greater than the bust measure, slant these lines outward instead of inward, this will necessitate a seam.

Fold the paper under on line *3*, and cut the pattern on the heavy outside lines.

HINTS FOR A PLAIN BASQUE.

There are over four hundred different systems of dress-drafting used in the United States, and any one of these to be of use requires constant practice.

Patterns are now easily obtained, and by using judgment and following the given directions carefully, will be found of great assistance. Patterns allowing for seams are easier to cut from, than those which do not.

The trimmings needed for a plain basque are linings, sewing silk, button-hole twist, basting cotton, buttons or hooks and eyes, and whale-bones.

The main parts of a plain basque pattern are front, back, side-back, under-arm, collar, upper-sleeve, and under-sleeve.

The front pattern can be distinguished from the back pattern by the shape of the neck and arm-scye, the neck of the front being cut lower, and the arm-scye being cut larger and having more of a curve. The upper-sleeve portion is wider than the under-sleeve portion, in order to bring the seams more under the arms.

The edge of the hem of the opening should be laid on the selvedge, to avoid making two folds in the hem.

Great care must be taken to baste the seams of a basque according to the marks ; few beginners realize that the difference of an eighth of an inch in the width of the seven seams, around the waist, will amount to one and three-fourths inches. Even basting stitches should be used. After the basque is basted, try it on. Alterations for tightening or loosening the basque, around the waist, should be made at the under-arm seams.

After the seams are sewed, take out the bastings ; pare the seams, making notches at the waist-line, and two inches above the waist-line, to allow for the curving of the dress. The under-arm seams may be left wider than the others, that the basque may be let out.

Press the seams open. Overcast the seams closely, or bind them with a narrow silk binding obtainable for this purpose.

Whale-bone casings can be bought, or a bias strip of silesia can be sewed on to the seams, fulling it a little. Soak the whale-bones in hot water for an hour, before using, which will render them soft and pliable enough to sew through. They should be firmly fastened an inch above and an inch below the waist-line.

To finish the lower edge of the basque, baste a bias strip of plain lining muslin, two inches wide, on the edge of the basque ; then fold the edges over half-an-inch, and catch them to the lining, fastening securely at the seams. Put on a facing of a thin material cut on the bias.

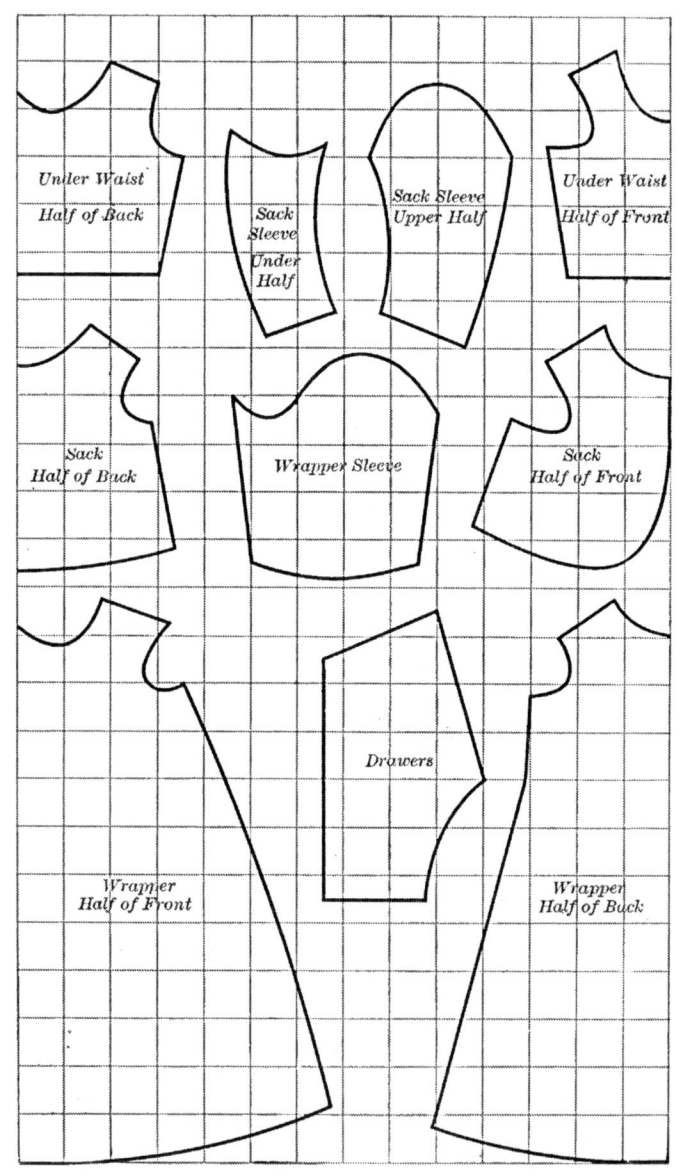

Fig. 111. — Doll's patterns.

DOLL'S PATTERNS.

On page 158, patterns are given for doll's garments. By using inch squared paper, and drawing the patterns in the same proportion, as they are given in the one-fourth inch squares, patterns will be obtained for a doll ten inches long.

TEACHER'S SUPPLEMENT.

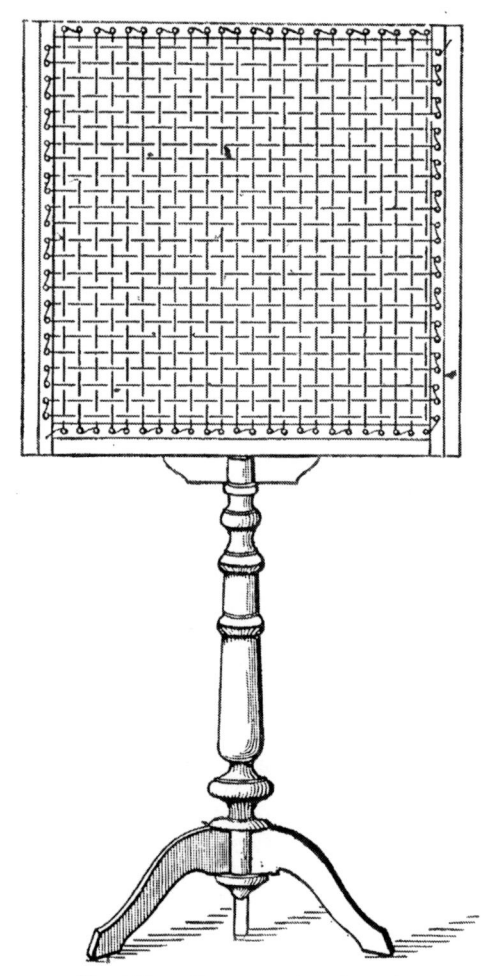

Fig. 112. — Demonstration Frame.

TEACHING THE LESSONS.

Every pupil should be thoroughly instructed in the meaning of general phrases; as, "work towards you," "from you," "from right to left," "threads of the cloth," etc. When dimensions are given, each pupil should be able to show on the cloth the different distances required; the depth of the little finger-nail may be referred to, when a fourth of an inch is needed.

Drills are necessary in teaching beginners the motions required in sewing, and should be given before beginning a new stitch. They interest the children, and promote dexterity and skillfulness. Children are apt to close their fingers when learning to sew, this may be obviated by the needle drill. The monotony of this may be made pleasant by calling it "shooting the needle," and allowing the children to aim the needle towards their neighbors. Drills for creasing hems and folding tucks and plaits may be practised on paper. The pupils who are proficient may be allowed to proceed with their work, while the others stand and practise the drill.

Simultaneous teaching. — In the instruction of classes, especially if they are large, good results can be obtained by simultaneous teaching. Class work is more effectual than individual work; the lesson being as easily dictated to a class of fifty, as to a single pupil.

Demonstration lessons are a great help in simultaneous teaching. On page 162 is an illustration of a frame used in European countries; smaller frames, that fasten on to the desk, are also used. The cords represent the threads of the cloth, and a large bone needle is used. In this country the frame has not proved very satisfactory. In its place, a piece of Java or coarse canvas, coarse heavy scrim, or linen crash may be hung over a wire on the wall or blackboard, or held in the hands. One advantage of the use of cloth is that it can be easily taken to any part of the room.

The stitch should be worked on the cloth in plain view of all the pupils. To give the exact position of the work, as it is held by the pupil, let the teacher stand with her back towards the pupils, and hold her hands at one side or above her head. A large needle and coarse, bright-colored yarn or twine should be used, so that the stitch can be easily seen ; in a large room this may be accomplished by repeating the demonstration on the opposite side of the room.

When approaching a new stitch, it is wise to spend a short time for several preceding lessons in simply showing how the stitch is taken.

The lesson may be divided into five parts : first, a talk on the subject matter, for instance, in a lesson on button-holes, describe the button-hole, its use, size, position, etc., also show garments having the required stitch; second, a demonstration lesson on the cloth, making the stitches very large and describing each motion ; third, an examination of the pupils concerning the talk and demonstration ; fourth, the demonstration repeated, having the pupils dictate the motions and the stitch ; fifth, all the pupils make the stitch on their trial-pieces, at the same time that it is again being demonstrated on the cloth. The next stitches may be made by following a pupil's dictation, the teacher showing how to move the cloth as the work progresses. Thus, by close attention and following the motions, the pupils learn the stitch; individual help will necessarily have to be given to the dull pupils.

These lessons require time and patience, but the results fully compensate. Teachers are apt to expect too much, and although it may seem as if little had been accomplished in the lesson hour, do not be discouraged, for, if the class has learned a little thoroughly, much has been gained. The pupil requires much practice on the simple stitches, but after the stitches are thoroughly learnt, rapid progress may be expected. A few fine garments made by the most capable pupils do not compensate for poor execution by the remainder of the class.

A teacher's success depends much on the first impressions given to her pupils. The *first lesson* should be a simple talk between teacher and pupils, in which the confidence of the pupils should be gained. This may be done by questioning them on the advantages and pleasures of learning to sew, outlining their course, pointing out the results, describing the articles required, etc. Let the first lesson be simply a preparation for a pleasant course.

The *second* lesson should be on the general directions, with explanations and oral instruction. At the close of each lesson the pupils should be able to answer the printed questions. It is a good plan to review the lessons at various times, by re-asking the questions.

The *third* and perhaps *fourth* lesson should be devoted to needles and thread, so that the pupils may become perfectly familiar with them, their size, location, and use.

The tying of the knot should be taught carefully, and each pupil should understand its construction, as many think a wad of thread is a knot. To accomplish this, let each pupil pass before the teacher with the thread partially drawn up, as in Fig. 1, and complete it under her oversight. This teaches also the proper size for the knot at the end of the thread. The directions for making the knot are given for the left hand, but children will often make it more readily with the right hand. Some teachers never allow the use of knots, except when absolutely necessary, while others consider it proper to use them, when they can be concealed. The fastening of the thread securely, in both beginning and ending, should be emphasized.

Circumstances and the teacher's judgment will decide the exact order in which the stitches should be taught, and which will vary according to the pupils' previous instruction in the kindergarten and primary schools. Some teachers prefer to begin with basting, others with running, but stitching, although harder, drills the pupils more in exactness.

Trial-piece. — The pupils, when learning, should always have a sample of the required stitch. A convenient trial-piece for the lower classes is prepared, by basting together the edges of two strips of cloth, one, eighteen inches by fourteen inches, the other, eighteen inches by four inches. A sample of stitching, two inches long, is placed under the basting, above which is a sample of overcasting. A narrow hem is basted on the opposite side of the broad piece, with a sample of hemming, also a sample of coarse button-hole stitch on the fold of the hem at the opposite corner; a basted seam for overhanding is two inches from the hem, with a sample of overhanding. On the narrow piece of cloth is a sample of running. Different colored thread should be used for each stitch.

A basting lesson may be given below the row of basting, and used for practice in stitching, followed by lessons in gathering, half-backstitching, etc. The trial-pieces may be prepared by the pupils of the higher grades. It is advisable to have different shaped trial-pieces for different grades, the older classes preparing their own pieces. The trial-pieces show the pupils' ability and proficiency.

How to keep the pupils busy. — If for any cause the pupils cannot sew on a garment or their regular work, they should work on their trial-pieces. The pupils will endeavor to do their best, if the work is to be kept for exhibition.

Thread. — On the trial-piece, different colored threads may represent degrees of advancement, or a different color may be used for each month's work, by which it may be easily perceived how much has been accomplished in the time. The joining of the thread in the different stitches should be shown by using different colors.

Stitches. — The check of gingham is of assistance to the pupils when learning, as they may be instructed to make a definite number of stitches in each check. The warp and woof of cloth may be distinguished by stretching the edges, that which stretches the least being the warp. Java canvas is excellent where threads are to be counted or drawn. It is better to teach *creasing* on a lengthwise strip of cloth, as it will not stretch. When the cloth has to be folded crosswise or on the bias, plaiting and pinching should be used. *Basting* may be easily taught on plaided or striped materials. In basting, where there will be no strain, the thread may be fastened by taking a few stitches one above the other; thus the thread can be easily picked out. In turning a narrow *hem*, explain that the first fold must not be quite as deep as the second fold, in order that it may lie smoothly.

Overcasting is difficult for children to do nicely, and may be taught on a folded edge. The proportions in the directions for overcasting are given in eighths and quarters of an inch, as they are convenient for the pupils to follow. Overcasting is often done from left to right. In *running* and *gathering* advanced pupils may be taught to keep the needle in the cloth until the seam is finished, pushing the gathers off the eye of the needle as the work proceeds. Explain to the pupils the difference in the use of *gathering* and *plaiting*, and that plaiting is used when it is desirable for the fulness to lie flat. Also show, by very coarse gathering, why the longest stitches are on the right side. The strips prepared in the lessons on gathering may be used for those on *bindings*.

In teaching the *button-hole stitch* on a folded edge, to young pupils, the following suggestions may be helpful: have the pupils point in the direction towards which they are to work; have them hold up their left hand, then their left forefinger; bring the folded edge of the cloth across the back of the fingers, allowing the tips to show; and hold the end of the fold between the left thumb and forefinger. After the stitch has been learned, it may be practised on a circle of flannel with bright-colored thread or twist. A lesson may be given on working an *uncut button-hole*, colored thread representing the sides of the slit; this is particularly helpful in teaching the working of the ends. When *barring* a button-hole, *after* overcasting, a short stitch taken at the middle of each side will keep the barring in position.

Whipping is one of the hardest class lessons ; the difference between rolling and folding should be demonstrated on large pieces of paper. *Darning* may be easily taught on canvas. A fine quality of flannel is a good material for cloth darning, as it is soft and yielding, and does not ravel. In *patching*, as it is sometimes difficult for the pupils to cut the hole in the garment by a thread, they may mark around a square cardboard pattern with a pencil, and, after cutting, ravel the edges until they are even. Care must be taken to place the edges of the cardboard parallel to the threads of the cloth. Marking cloth with a lead-pencil should not be encouraged, as the marks are hard to wash out ; when it is necessary to use a pencil, a blue one is preferable. After teaching *feather-stitching* on canvas, a striped material will serve as a guide for the pupil. On *canvas-work*, crochet cord, apothecary twine, or common twine split may be used instead of worsted. In teaching *marking*, it is a good plan to have the pupils draw the letters first.

Drafting and cutting may be given by demonstration lessons. The pupils should not draft or cut a dress-waist until they have had experience on underclothing or simpler patterns.

The garment should be shown the pupils and its proportions explained before drafting, and instruction given as to the amount of cloth required, the width of the material, etc. Instruction should also be given on choosing materials and patterns suitable to the form of the person, and the use of the garment. For instance, a tall person should not wear stripes or plaits, nor a short person large plaids or many ruffles. Fulness is becoming to a thin form, and dark colors apparently decrease the size of a fleshy person.

Where measurements are given, as in the child's drawers, call a pupil of appropriate size forward, and take the measures before the school.

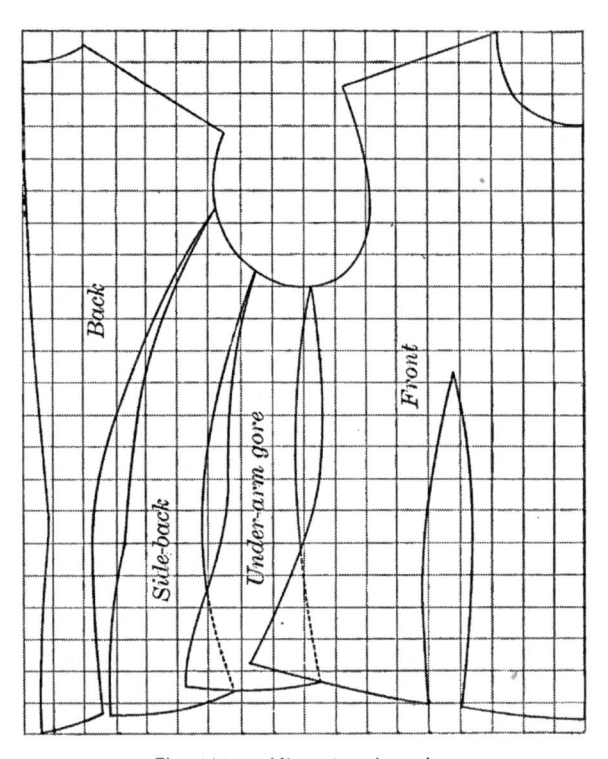

Fig. 113. — Misses' underwaist.

Fig. 113 represents a Misses' underwaist, bust measure thirty-two inches. By re-drawing in one-inch squares the exact size (not allowing for seams) will be obtained, and may be used as a demonstration lesson to show the different parts of a waist, their size, shape, and proportion, also to show how the parts should join ; notches may be made at the waist-line or at the top as preferred.

Squared paper is of great assistance in drafting; a miniature pattern may be drawn by using fourth-of-an-inch squares as inch squares, thus giving the pupils the proportions of the garment. Doll's patterns are convenient, as they take up less room, yet give the pupils the shape and proportions of the garment, and show how the seams should be placed together. One of the first lessons in cutting may be a doll's two-breadth apron, cut from old exercise paper; the paper may also be used for the bib.

The pupils should be allowed to take home the patterns they draft, as they are appreciated by the parents.

Many teachers think that dress drafting should be taught in the last part of the High School course or in the Normal School. If younger pupils are taught a system of drafting, they often have not sufficient judgment to apply the knowledge gained

COURSE OF SEWING.

The following course of sewing, drafting and cutting has been found practical in a grammar school course of six years, but it may be re-arranged and adapted to a shorter course.

FIRST YEAR.

Position of the pupils while sewing.

Method of threading needle, making a knot, and using the thimble.

Drills.

Basting.

Coarse button-hole stitch on a folded edge of cloth.

Overcasting.

Running.

Stitching.

Turning, basting and hemming one-fourth of an inch hems.

Practice in cutting and putting together a paper or cloth sample of a two-breadth apron.

Instruction on the use of needles, thread, thimbles and cloth.

Examination.

Suitable articles to make. — Bags, towels, sewing aprons, drawers and two-breadth aprons.

SECOND YEAR.

Review.

Fine button-hole stitch on a folded edge of cloth.

French hem on damask.

Gathering, and placing of gathers.

Half-backstitching.

Overhanding.
Putting on bands by stitching and hemming.
Running and a backstitch.
Turning, basting and hemming one-inch hems.
Practice in drafting and cutting pockets and child's bib.
Instruction on the manufacture of needles, thimbles and emery.
Examination.
Suitable articles to make. — Skirts, drawers, aprons, doll's clothes, sheets, pillow-cases and table-linen.

THIRD YEAR.

Review.
Blanket-stitch.
Button-holes in cotton cloth.
Buttons.
Catch-stitch.
Darning a straightway tear or cut in cotton cloth.
Double gathering.
French seam.
Lace sewed on.
Loops.
Plackets.
Practice in weaving.
Wide hems.
Practice in drafting and cutting a night-dress yoke and child's drawers.
Instruction on the manufacture of scissors, pins, buttons, hooks and eyes.
Examination.
Suitable articles to make. — Dresses, night-dresses, flannel skirts, etc.

FOURTH YEAR.

Review.
Bias piecing.
Button-holes in woollen cloth.
Chain-stitch.
Darning a bias and a corner-tear.
Darning on s ockinet.
Double gathering overhanded to a band.
Facings.
Gussets.
Hooks and eyes.
Loops of tape.
Outline-stitch.
Patching on cotton cloth.
Plaiting.
Scalloped edge.
Shirring.
Straightway fell.

Practice in drafting and cutting a gored skirt and child's tier.

Instruction on the growth and manufacture of thread, cotton and wool.

Examination.

FIFTH YEAR.

Review.
Bias-fell.
Corners mitred.
Darning tear in woollen cloth with silk, ravellings or hair.
Edgings sewed on and corners turned.
Embroidery knots.
Eyelet-holes.

Feather-stitch.
Gathers set into a band.
Grafting.
Hem-stitch.
Honey-combing.
Marking.
Patching on calico, gingham and woollen cloth.
Piping.
Ruffles faced on.
Slip or blind-stitch.
Stocking-web stitch.
Tucking.
Whipping.
Practice in drafting and cutting drawers and child's waist.

Instruction on the growth and manufacture of silk and linen.

Examination.

SIXTH YEAR.

Review.

Drafting, cutting and making of garments, also cutting from patterns.

Examination.

PRACTICAL SUGGESTIONS.

Although teachers may have different methods in regard to details; those presented in the lessons have been found to be practical for service, and easily acquired by the pupils.

In beginning with a class of young pupils, close attention should be given to the details, or the bright, intelligent pupil alone will comprehend. In an average class, one-fourth are quick to learn, one-half are of average ability, and the remaining fourth may be called dull. A teacher should not judge the proficiency of the class by either extreme. The best work does not always represent the greatest effort. Poor work may be excusable in some cases, especially from pupils who have come from homes of ignorance and poverty.

The spirit of the pupils depend greatly upon the disposition of the teacher. A smiling face will often accomplish more than severe words. Commendation for worthy efforts helps the pupils wonderfully, and care should be taken not to discourage the dull pupils.

Experience teaches that a child, when working on a real object of use, not only does better work, but gets more good from it, through the arousing of interest and the developing of self-respect, than when simply practising stitches. The principle of working with a definite aim is important, though trial-pieces are necessary at first, for a child should not be allowed to spoil a garment, or think that poor sewing will do if only the garment can be put together. An incentive to the child to do her best on the trial-piece, is the knowledge that she may apply the acquired skill to some useful article. The child should not be discouraged by being required to practise longer than is necessary. After she has done as well as she is able, allow her to bring from home an unmade garment requiring the necessary stitches. The pupils may be stimulated in stitching, by the promise that they may outline their names or some design on cloth. As a reward for good work, the pupils may be allowed to dress dolls, or have their work mounted and labelled for exhibition. Pupils will often learn readily from a companion, and those who first learn the stitches may be permitted to aid the others, and also to show their work, if done nicely, to the class.

Dark days. — Teachers should be careful that the pupils do not strain their eyes by working in a poor light. On dark days, talks, which are of great assistance and benefit may be given on relevant subjects, as needles, thread, cotton, wool, silk and linen, their manufacture and use (see page 222), and on the making of garments. A dark day may also be employed in teaching the pupils to make knots, including square and bow-knots.

A shopping expedition will greatly interest the pupils, for instance : — " What kind of a store shall we visit to purchase our sewing materials?" "What shall we buy?" "How much material shall we get for a bag, apron or skirt?" "What kind of material?" "Why?" "Are we ready to go home?" "O, no, we must have other things." Mention them ; tell why different numbers of needles are needed for different materials, etc. Question on the difference in the quality of materials, and explain that a good quality is generally cheaper in the end.

178   SCHOOL NEEDLEWORK.

Fancy-work. — In the public schools embroidery or fancy-work is not generally encouraged; but a little attention given to it before Christmas is greatly enjoyed by the children. They may be allowed to bring the presents they are preparing, or class lessons may be given on the making of needle-books, pin-balls, scissors and thimble cases, etc. Lessons on tissue paper work afford much pleasure, and here is an opportunity for a practical lesson on the combination of colors. Simple embroidery may be taught. Fig. 114 represents a scalloped embroidered edge, which is easily acquired by a pupil who has practised the blanket-stitch.

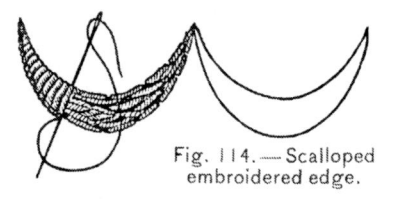

Fig. 114. — Scalloped embroidered edge.

Scissors. — It is not advisable for young pupils to have scissors in their bags, as they lack judgment in their use. Class scissors should be kept in a strong box lined with felt or velvet. Pupils may practise cutting on paper to advantage, so as to become accustomed to the use of scissors. When many button-holes of the same length are to be cut, the annoyance caused by the ends of the scissors catching in the cloth, or by the screw loosening, may be prevented by soldering the screw at the required length.

Dropping articles. — To prevent the disturbance caused by dropping articles, have the pupils keep their spools, emery, etc., in their bags during the sewing lesson.

Sinistrous pupils. — The broadening of the popular mind begins to change many formerly fixed opinions. One of these is in regard to the left hand. Formerly a sinistrous person was considered an oddity. Now, instead of teaching the exclusive use of the right hand, left-handed pupils are taught the use of both, as an ambidextrous person has many advantages over a person confined to the use of one hand. Fig. 115 represents the needle and thread in position for working a button-hole with the left hand.

Sampler. — To make a sampler similar to Fig. 116, a piece of cotton cloth twenty-four inches long and eighteen inches wide is required.

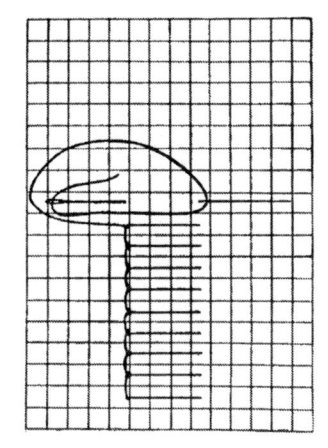

Fig. 115. — Button-hole worked with the left hand.

Make a narrow hem at the sides. At the middle of the lower edge cut in seven or eight inches, hem the opening, and set-in a gusset.

At the right-hand lower edge hem-stitch an inch hem; above make two tucks one-fourth of an inch deep, the first tuck sewed with a running stitch, the second tuck with a running and a backstitch; then make a narrow straightway fell. Sew a whipped, cambric ruffle, trimmed with Hamburg edging, to the lower edge of the hem.

Tear off one inch from the left-hand lower edge, and face on a cambric ruffle, having a lace edge; hemstitch the facing. Above make two tucks one-fourth of an inch deep, the first tuck sewed by stitching, the second tuck by half-backstitching; then make a narrow French seam. Fasten the opening with a hook and eye, placed at the middle of the edges of the hems; back of the eye place a loop for a fastening.

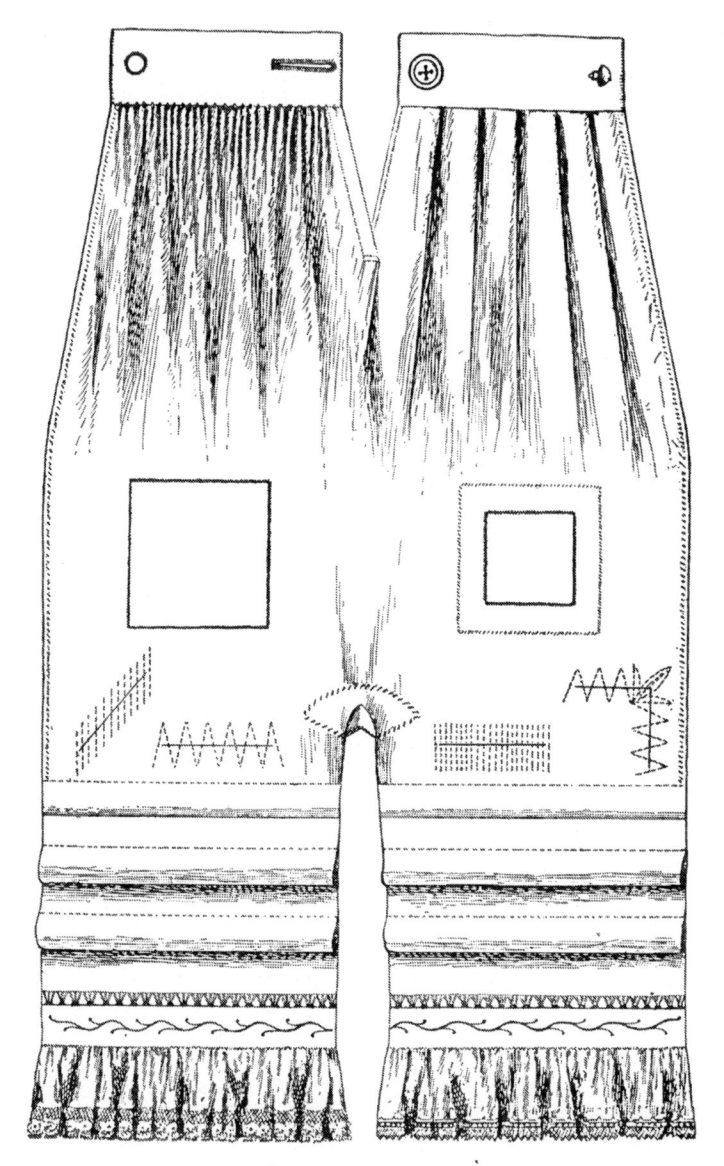

Fig. 116.—Sampler.

Above the fell and French seam darn two straightway-tears, one with vertical, and one with slanting stitches ; also a bias-tear and a corner-tear. Above the darns sew a patch by hemming, and one by overhanding, overcasting the edges of the latter. Chain-stitch a vine on the lower inch hem, and outline a similar vine on the opposite side. Decorate the vines with embroidery knots.

At the middle of the upper edge make a placket four inches deep. On one of the edges put on a binding by setting-in or by overhanding, making a row of double gathering. Plait the opposite side, and put on a binding by stitching and hemming. Fasten the placket with a four-holed button and a button-hole. Make an eyelet-hole at one of the outer ends of the bindings, and sew a boot-button at the opposite end. Above the four-holed button a loop of tape may be sewed.

A flannel patch, with the edges blanket-stitched, and samples of stockinet darning may be tacked on to the sampler. The name may be worked from the alphabets on a piece of scrim, the edges finished by feather-stitching, and then tacked to the sampler.

If desired, the different methods of basting may be shown on the tucks.

Blackboard. — A blackboard should be divided by light-colored lines, into inch squares, using a different color for every ninth or twelfth line. A permanent blackboard may be made by marking out the squares with paint. If there is a lack of blackboard room for this, mounted blackboard-cloth may be prepared, and hung on the wall or placed on an easel. The use of the blackboard is of great assistance in impressing upon the pupils the size and form of the stitches, and in teaching the dimensions in cutting.

Drawing lessons should be given in connection with sewing; they serve not only as a means for teaching the stitches, but also assist in training the eye and the hand.

A free-hand diagram, drawn on the blackboard by the teacher, in connection with the demonstration lesson, will

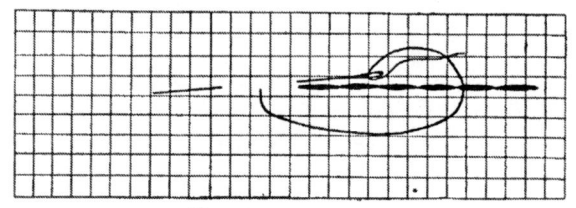

Fig. 117. — Stitching.

excite the interest and gain the attention of the pupils. The name of the lesson should be plainly written on the blackboard. The copying of the diagram by the pupils

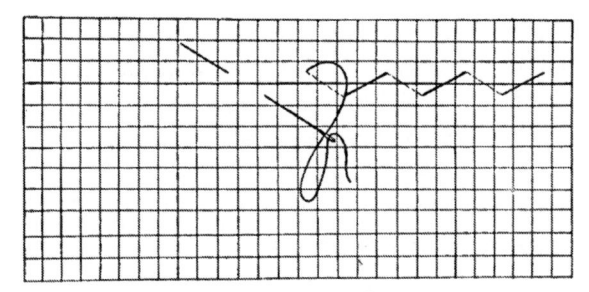

Fig. 118. — Hemming.

will be found very effectual in teaching the size, regularity and proportion of the stitches. After a little practice and help the pupils will be able to draw more difficult stitches, and give simple sketches of their work; thereby exercising their judgment and taste.

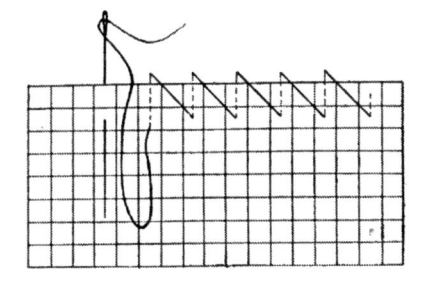

Fig. 119.—Overhanding.

To aid teachers, who are not accustomed to free-hand drawing, the diagram may be marked out previous to the lesson with black crayon or a soft slate-pencil; if this is done lightly it will not be perceptible to the pupils.

By following this plan the different points of the lesson can be easily illustrated, as the lesson proceeds; and it has been found more effectual than a previously completed drawing.

Figures 117 to 121 are given as simple diagrams suitable to be drawn on the blackboard. They can be easily enlarged by re-drawing them in inch squares. The lines represent the threads of the cloth. Different colored chalk should be used in representing the joining of the thread; two colors are also necessary in marking to plainly show that the stitches are crossed in the same direction.

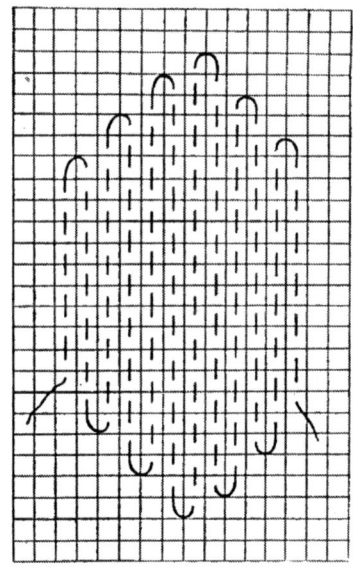

Fig. 120.—Darning a thin place in cloth.

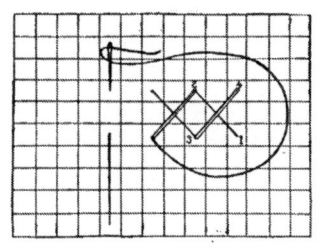

Fig. 121. — Marking.

When giving a lesson on drawing the stitches or garment, squared paper or sectional exercise books will be found helpful; children will also be interested, if allowed to draw the stitches on the blackboard.

Compositions. — The various forms of manual training furnish subjects for language work, both oral and written, and sewing as a distinct and recognized form of manual training, should receive, from both the sewing teacher and the class teacher, attention as a means for the expression of thought in composition work. Compositions should be required on topics selected from the various subjects in the sewing lessons. The topics for the lower classes may be given on the different stitches, and for the older classes, on drafting, cutting and making of garments. "The benefits derived from a knowledge of sewing," "the source and manufacture of materials used in sewing," "history of a garment," and kindred subjects may be suggested as additional topics, according to the line of work pursued.

If the pupils have taken drawing in connection with sewing, they will be able to illustrate their compositions. The compositions should be looked over by the sewing teacher to determine the correctness of the knowledge of the pupils.

Examinations. — Oral or written examinations may be given; if the latter, they may take the form of a composition. The preparation of the trial-piece is a good test in regard to the simple stitches.

Exhibitions. — An exhibition at the close of the year's work is a great incentive, especially when all the sewing of the year, from the trial-pieces to the cut and made garments of all descriptions, is exhibited.

Mounting models. — The models obtained from the lessons may be mounted for exhibition in a kindergarten mounting-book or a scrap-book. An inexpensive book may be made of manilla paper, securing the leaves together with ribbons or fasteners, and made attractive by a bright cover. A class-banner may be made of the models by sewing them together, then lining and mounting them. The models may also be mounted on a strip of cardboard, folded backward and forward, the last fold being doubled over the others. Sample models from each class may be arranged on a large sheet of cardboard, with the pupils' names written on labels. Inexpensive stands may be made for the exhibiting of dresses, by fastening a standard, in the form of a cross, into a solid block of wood. The cross-bar for the shoulders of the dress may be straight or curved. For a child's dress, the block of wood should be eight inches square, the upright thirty inches high, and the cross-bar eleven inches wide. For a larger dress, the block should be ten inches square, the upright fifty inches high, and the cross-piece seventeen inches wide.

Boys' sewing. — Boys are now being taught sewing in the lower classes of many of the public schools, and it has been found helpful in forming habits of quietness, neatness and accuracy, besides teaching them to repair their clothes. Boys are not generally immaculate, and colored materials are more satisfactory than white. To interest boys there must be a great variety in the work.

A successful teacher of boys begins by teaching the stitches on colored canvas, following with a small checked gingham bag, three or more stitches being taken in each check. Then they learn the sewing-on of buttons; a gingham apron made for mother; a flannel blouse; splashers; darning, first on canvas or cardboard, then on cloth; patching; the working of the alphabet and figures on canvas, etc. An interesting outline map may also be made, by tracing the map on paper and pricking the outline on drab cambric; the pricking is done with a coarse needle over a piece of heavy cardboard or felt. The land may be outlined with white knitting cotton, the rivers with finer cotton, the mountains represented by the knot-stitch, the principle cities located with red embroidery cotton, etc. Animals or any outline picture may be traced on cambric.

Collection of work. — At the close of each lesson, the work should be collected in such a manner that it may be readily distributed. This may be done by having a large bag for each row, always beginning to collect at one end, and to distribute at the other.

The waste-basket should be passed at the end of the sewing lesson for the scraps of thread, etc.

KINDERGARTEN SEWING.

Sewing over outlines pricked on cards gives profitable variety to manual work. The object of this kind of work is various. By it the child acquires the use of the needle. He becomes familiar with the elements of form, the different lines, angles and geometric figures, and by constantly working with them according to certain laws of harmony and arrangement, he is enabled to apply these laws in the expression of new forms, fostering the inventive and artistic sense. The child's sense of color is developed, as he is guided by the teacher in the selection of colors, and is shown wherein they blend harmoniously. The sewing serves also as a most efficient means for illustrating any subject under consideration.

This work assists in training the character, by the exercise of the child's three-fold nature, physical, mental and moral. Physically he gains control of his muscles and acquires dexterity. His mental power of observation is trained by the close observance required in the proper representation of surrounding objects. His moral being is developed by the necessity of exactness, patience and care, and by the privilege that the child has of giving of his efforts in the form of the simple little things that he makes.

The first lesson in kindergarten sewing should not exceed half-an-hour in length, and may be given on working with worsted a circle perforated on a card. The teacher should be furnished with long-eyed, blunt-pointed needles, and a thread-case filled with split zephyr, silk, or coarse sewing cotton (the latter can be obtained at a kindergarten supply store). Before the lesson the teacher should have all preparations completed, the needles threaded with short lengths of worsted, which is tied into the needle to prevent its becoming unthreaded, the circle pricked on the cards, and the work begun.

A simple explanations should precede the work, telling what is to be done; why the knot is on the under side; what we will call the circle, e.g. let us call this circle a path, and build a fence on it, so that we may keep our sheep inside, or some other simple illustration to arouse the interest and lend a zest to the work. Now show the pupil how to put the needle down through one hole, which hides the point; let him look for the point, which he finds by turning over the card; bring the point up through the next hole, pointing it towards the ceiling. This explanation may be given in the form of a play of hide and seek, and must necessarily be repeated several times; individual attention should be given to each one. Before the work goes very far numerous accidents may occur, as the worsted breaking, the card tearing, etc., but we must remember that this is the first lesson, and the little fingers are entirely unaccustomed to such work, and a real effort is made by them. Before working around the second time, further illustrate, e.g. we have now partly finished our fence, but what are all these openings between the stitches? We must fill them in, by going around again, so our sheep cannot get out.

The advancement necessarily will be slow, but in time they will be able to follow any pricked line. The backward may be stimulated by praising the best work, and the reward of taking the cards home is a great incentive.

Encourage them to thread their own needles, using a few fibres of cotton-batting to cover the ends of the worsted; and also encourage them to fasten their thread; this is done by putting the needle into the nearest stitch on the wrong side, again putting the needle in, and leaving a loop, pass the needle through the loop, and draw closely.

Try to follow nature, as much as possible, in the selection of colors, as, work an apple with red or yellow, and have a brown stem.

A convenient case for holding the worsted, silk and cotton, cut into the required lengths, may be made by taking a piece of silesia (or any material) about twenty-seven inches long, and eighteen inches wide. Have a centre piece sixteen inches long and fourteen inches wide. Bind the edges of each piece, and stitch them together with rows of stitching one inch or less apart, according to the kind of thread to be placed in it. At one end place flannel leaves for needles, and at the other make a full pocket for odds and ends. When the lesson is through the ends may be folded over before rolling, and everything is secure.

It is well to allow the children to select their colors, draw the worsted from the case, and make their own combinations.

If the children do the pricking they need to be supplied with a pricking needle or a shawl pin, and a pad made of heavy felt, glued to cardboard. The holes should be one-eighth of an inch or farther apart.

Cards may be either stamped with the designs, or merely pricked. There should be a separate card for each series. When many copies of a design are needed, a cardboard pattern may be cut, and the design traced by

190   SCHOOL NEEDLEWORK.

it; or a hektograph may be used. The designs may also be reproduced by using tracing and impression paper. A pantograph is very convenient for enlarging or reducing designs.

TEACHER'S SUPPLEMENT. 191

The illustrations on pages 190 to 197 will give an idea of kindergarten work. Before beginning the regular series of linear sewing, the circular course (page 195) is generally given, thus expressing the ideas of the first gift

192   SCHOOL NEEDLEWORK.

lessons. Ideas of color may be further impressed by filling in the sewed forms with colored crayons.

Linear sewing, as illustrated on pages 190 to 194, begins with the simplest elements of all geometric forms or designs, and leads by combinations to complex figures in artistic work.

TEACHER'S SUPPLEMENT. 193

The 1st series embraces the vertical line, then its opposite, the horizontal; combinations making angles. Combinations of angles to make a border, stair pattern, etc. The geometric figure from the same angle follows; another combination makes the Greek cross.

2nd series. — Combinations of the same angles, part of the lines twice the length of the others.

3d series. — Combinations of vertical and horizontal lines of unequal length, the vertical twice the length of the horizontal.

4th series. — Combinations of vertical and horizontal lines, the horizontal twice the length of the vertical.

5th series. — The oblique line, and its combination into angles, borders and geometric figures.

6th series. — (No illustration.) Combinations of the vertical with the oblique of a square.

7th series. — (No illustration.) Combinations of the horizontal with the oblique of a square.

8th series. — Combinations of oblique lines of different lengths, one line twice the length of the other.

9th series. — Combinations of vertical, horizontal and oblique lines.

10th series. — Introduces the diagonal of a vertical oblong.

11th series. — Introduces the diagonal of a horizontal

oblong, and following patterns are given combining the elements of series 10 and 11.

12th series. — Combinations of vertical and horizontal lines of unequal length with oblique; the oblique being the diagonal of vertical oblong.

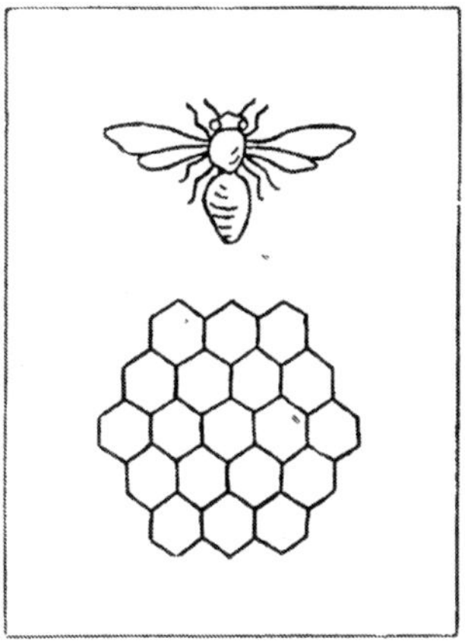

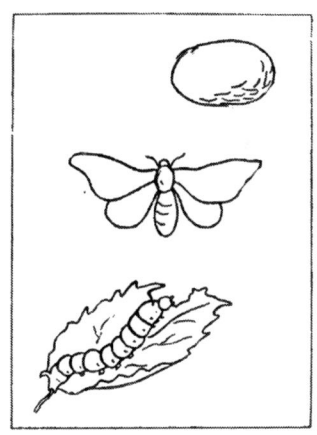

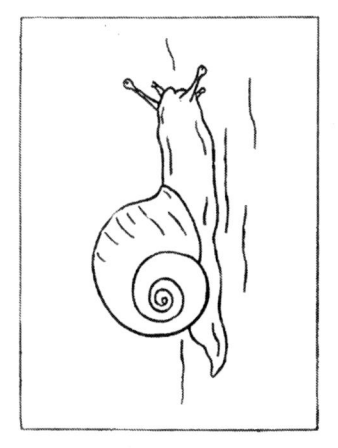

13th series. — Combinations of vertical and horizontal lines of unequal length with oblique ; the oblique being the diagonal of horizontal oblong.

14th series. — Equilateral triangles and their combinations.

Followed by more complex combinations leading to greater artistic efforts. The illustrations on page 196 represent the seedling maple, and the full-grown leaf; the apple leaf, bud, blossom and fruit. The illustrations on page 197 represents the bee and honey-comb; the cocoon, moth and silkworm; the snail and his shell; the bird and her nest. These may be enlarged (page 202), and used in connection with nature lessons.

PRIMARY SEWING.

The tactile sense, a child's sense of touch, should be developed from the very first, and should be cultivated throughout his entire course of education.

The methods of kindergarten teaching are based on this idea, and it should be continued in the primary and again in the grammar schools. One projection of this idea has been the adopting of clay modeling, paper folding, etc., in many primary schools. As the course advances, the rough, coarse materials should give place to finer ones; so the weaving of paper, sewing with embroidery needles and worsted on cardboard should be supplanted by finer needles and thread and the use of cloth. There should be no break between the sewing of the kindergarten and that of the grammar grades, especially as the knowledge gained in the primary facilitates and advances the work in the grammar.

No objection can be raised because of mixed classes, as experience teaches that primary sewing is enjoyed by boys as much as by girls, and prepares the boys for their manual work in the grammar school.

The educational value of sewing in the primary school is of more importance than the utility.

Educational Sewing Squares for Primary Work. — One of the various objections to primary sewing has been the difficulty in preparing useful and interesting work. The "Educational Sewing Squares" meet this difficulty. The designs are representations of objects and geometric forms, and in the sewing of them, the child not only

200 SCHOOL NEEDLEWORK.

learns the stitches, but becomes familiar with the forms. The child's eye and hand are trained by following the stitches which are plainly marked on the cloth, and thus the pupil is prepared for free-hand sewing. The work is pro-

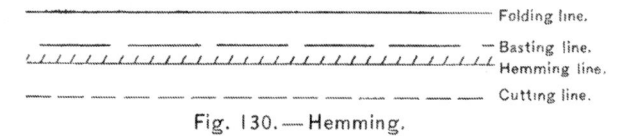

```
——————————————————————————— Folding line.
——  ——  ——  ——  ——  —— Basting line.
//////////////////////////// Hemming line.
——  ——  ——  ——  ——  ——  —— Cutting line.
```
Fig. 130.—Hemming.

gressive; and the squares, when finished, may be sewed together for a doll's table-covering or bed-spread.

The "Educational Sewing Squares" consist of a sheet of white cotton cloth, twenty-one by thirty-six inches, on which are stamped thirty-two designs, each design being

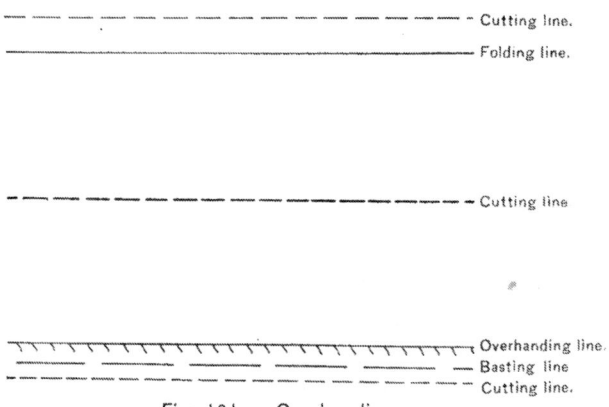

```
——  ——  ——  ——  ——  ——  —— Cutting line.
———————————————————————— Folding line.




——  ——  ——  ——  ——  ——  —— Cutting line.



\\\\\\\\\\\\\\\\\\\\\\\\\\ Overhanding line.
——  ——  ——  ——  —— Basting line.
——  ——  ——  ——  —— Cutting line.
```
Fig. 131.—Overhanding.

in a four-inch square. At the sides are strips for hemming and overhanding (for samples of which see Figures 130 and 131); lines for cutting, folding, creasing and basting are marked on each strip. At the upper side are four-holed buttons (Fig. 132). Above the strip of buttons is the title of the squares; to strengthen the cloth this should be folded under and basted, before sewing the buttons.

The squares are to be cut on the dash-lines. The edges of the first twenty-two squares are marked for overcasting (pages 204–214); the edges of the next two squares are for blanket-stitching (page 215); the next four squares may be either overcast or blanket-stitched (pages 216–217); and the last four squares are for free-hand sewing. The designs are to be sewed either by running or by stitching; there are three sizes of each stitch, the aim being progression.

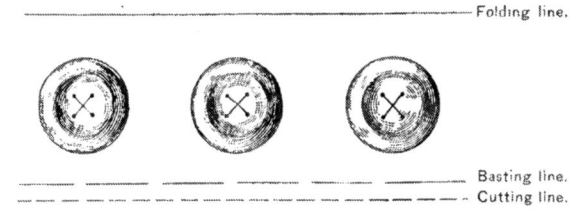

Fig. 132. — Buttons.

Lessons. — Sewing to a little child has a charm, because mamma does it. At first, especially if the child has not attended a kindergarten, it is difficult for the little hands to use the needle, thread, thimble and cloth; but the work is attractive, and in time the obstacles will be overcome.

The first lessons should be spent in teaching the position of the body, holding of the work, threading of the needle, wearing of the thimble, making knots, and fastening the thread (see General Directions). Explain the use of the eye and sharp point of the needle; and that the thimble is worn to protect the finger in pushing the needle through the cloth, the indentations holding the needle firmly. Exercise the children in distinguishing the right hand from the left. After supplying each child with a well-fitting thimble, have them find the longest finger of the right hand, and put the thimble on, pressing it with the thumb. The needle and thimble drill (page 14) should then follow. A drill on the stitch should be given before allowing the children to work that stitch on the squares.

As far as possible the squares should be sewed in connection with the form, study, drawing and color-work.

For a demonstration lesson (page 163) the design can be easily enlarged by dividing it into squares, and drawing in the design on the same number of larger squares.[1] For this purpose squared paper, with the squares from one-eighth of an inch to an inch in diameter, can be obtained at a kindergarten supply store. The enlarged design can be transferred to cloth by using impression paper. A large bone needle can be used on Java canvas; if this kind of a needle is not easily obtained, a netting-needle can be used by soldering the openings at the ends.

The length of time given to a lesson should depend upon the number of pupils; with a class of fifty pupils some teachers prefer to teach half the class for half the alloted time, while others think best to teach the entire class.

A coarse needle and coarse bright-colored thread are suitable for a beginner to use; finer ones may be used as the pupil advances. A fast-colored thread is necessary, as the squares will generally need washing after being

[1] It is necessary to enlarge the design many times, that the lines and dots may be plainly discerned from any part of the room.

sewed. Different colored thread may be used to show degrees of proficiency. Encourage the children to thread their needles, and as soon as they succeed, allow them to begin their work, or a little praise for success will incite the backward.

The work should be begun at an advantageous place, and long stitches should be avoided in passing from one point to another.

The first stitch taught is overcasting, as the first work done by the pupil is the overcasting of the edges of the squares to prevent their ravelling.

Puckering the work, especially in running, must be constantly guarded against. To aid in preventing this, explain that the work must be smoothed out every few stitches, and show, on a piece of cloth, how the work will pucker if the thread is drawn tightly.

The more advanced pupils may use the Kensington outline-stitch instead of stitching. A pretty square for the centre of the doll's table-covering or bed-spread may be made by hemming on a design or figure cut from cretonne or momie cloth. Some of the pupils in the higher classes may be able to make doll's garments, patterns of which may be obtained from page 158.

The distribution and collection of the work may be facilitated by having a separate box for each row; each child's name should be written on the back of the work, or the child may write its name on paper and pin the paper on to the work; then, if the work is collected systematically, it can be readily distributed at the next lesson. Some teachers prefer for each child to have a small bag, this avoids fitting thimbles at each lesson.

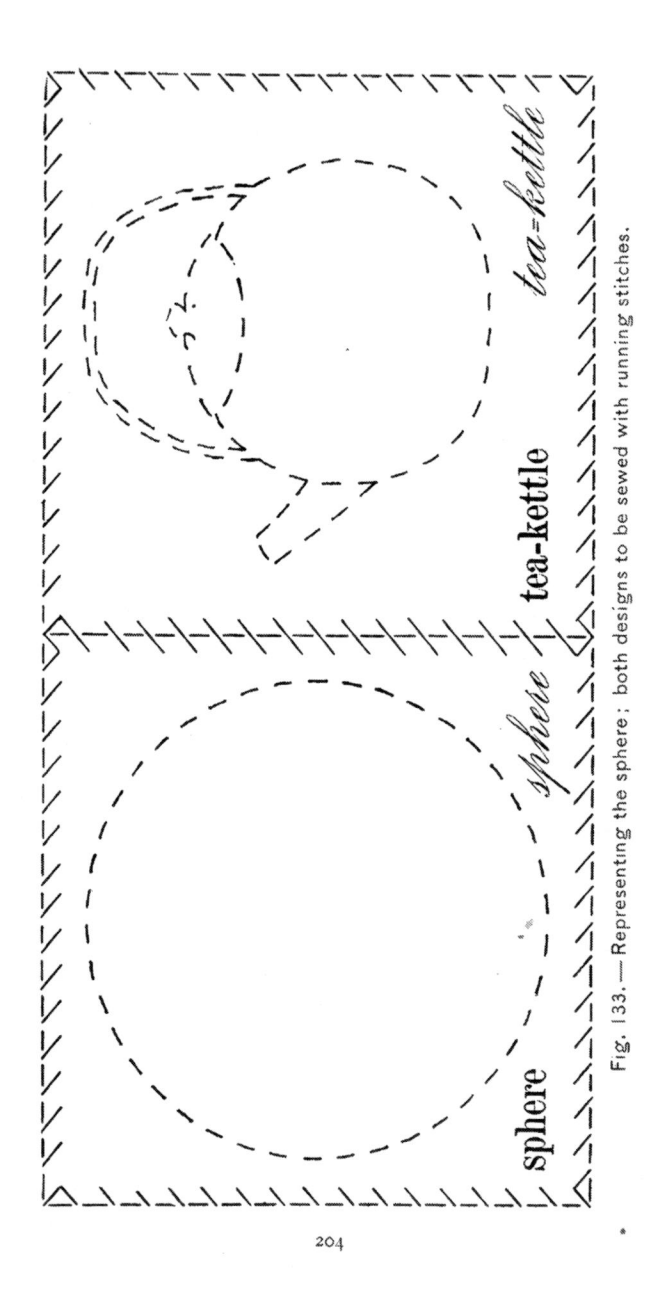

Fig. 133.— Representing the sphere; both designs to be sewed with running stitches.

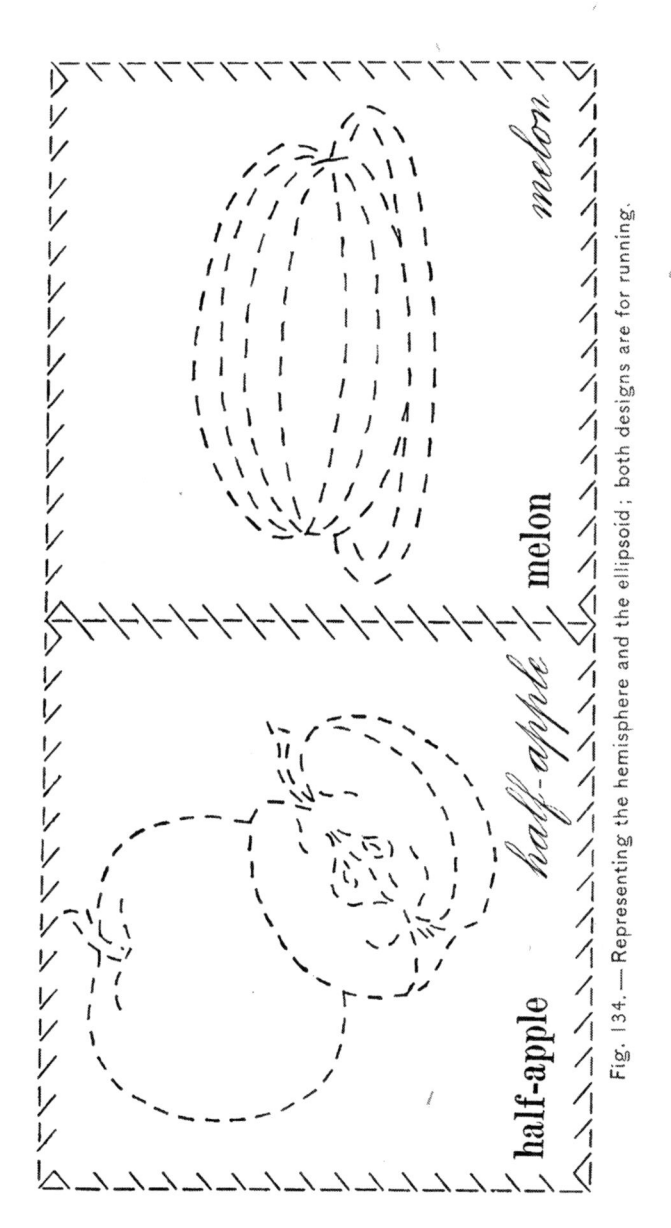

Fig. 134.—Representing the hemisphere and the ellipsoid; both designs are for running.

205

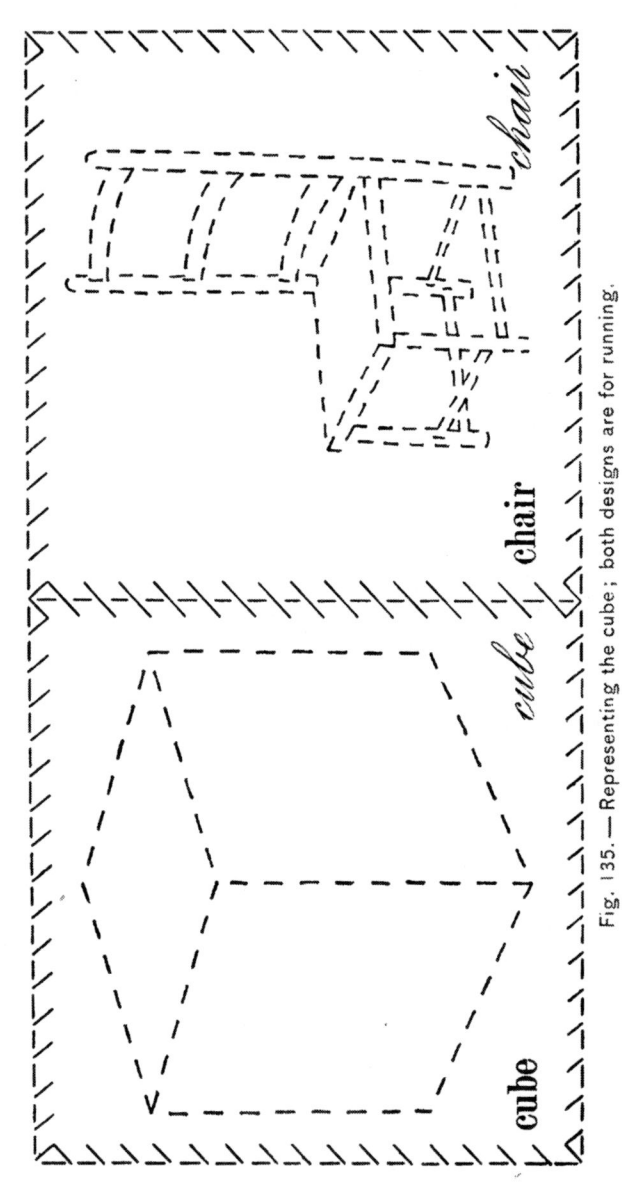

Fig. 135. — Representing the cube; both designs are for running.

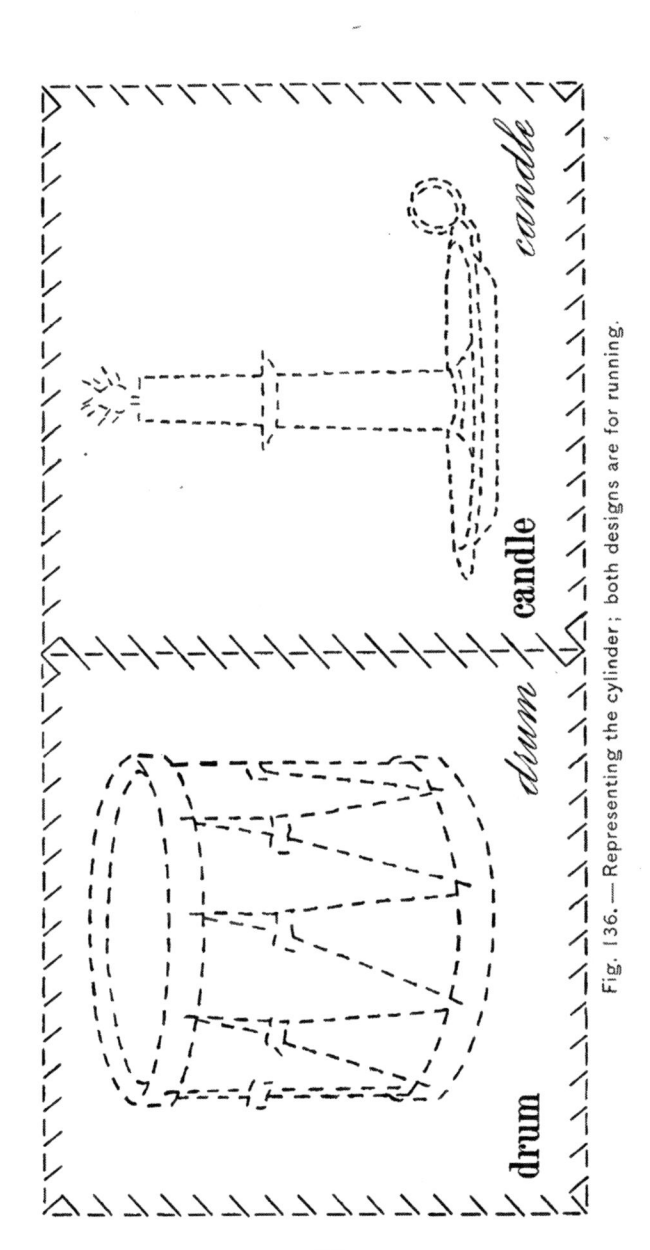

Fig. 136.—Representing the cylinder; both designs are for running.

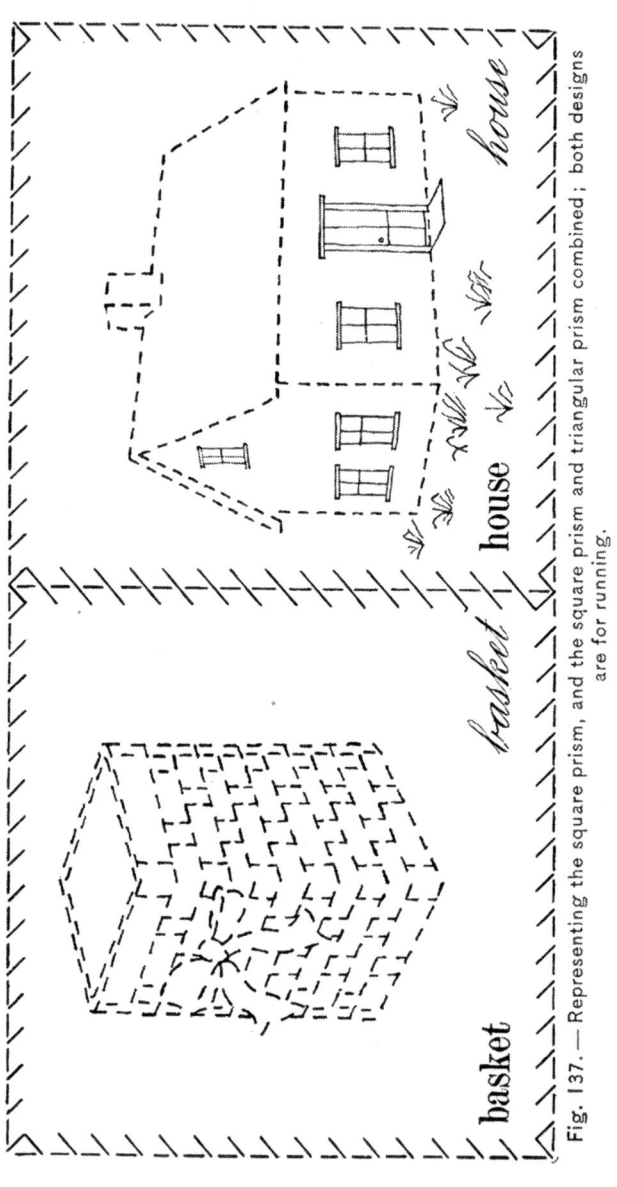

Fig. 137. — Representing the square prism, and the square prism and triangular prism combined; both designs are for running.

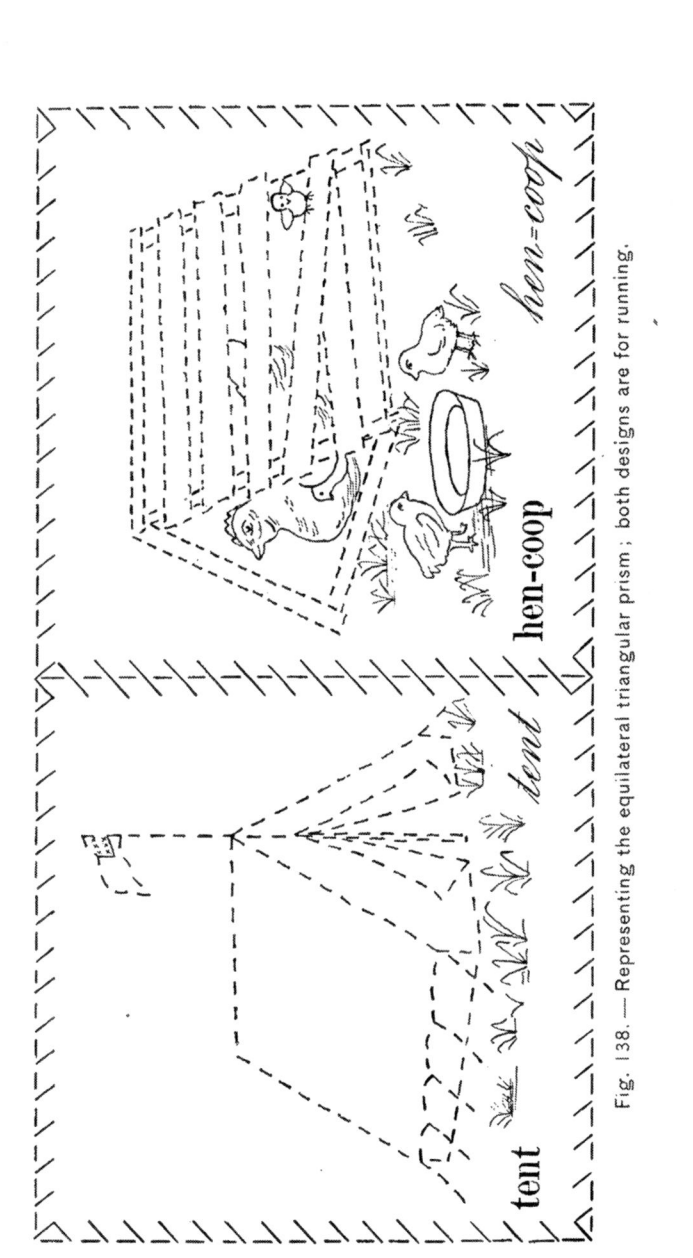

Fig. 138.—Representing the equilateral triangular prism; both designs are for running.

210

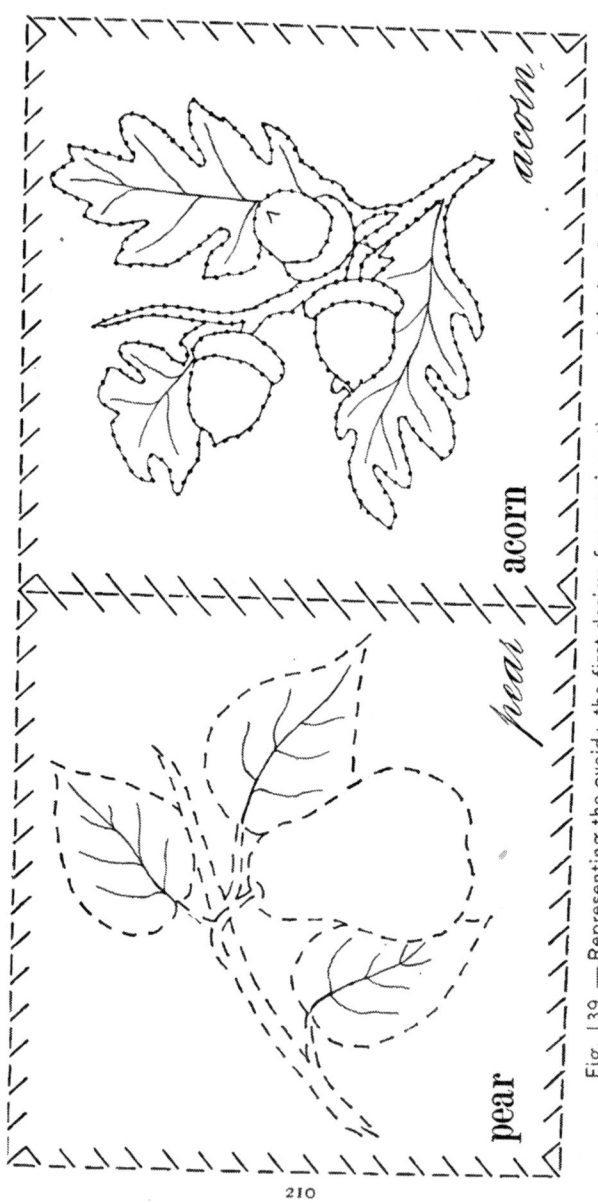

Fig. 139. — Representing the ovoid: the first design for running, the second design for stitching.

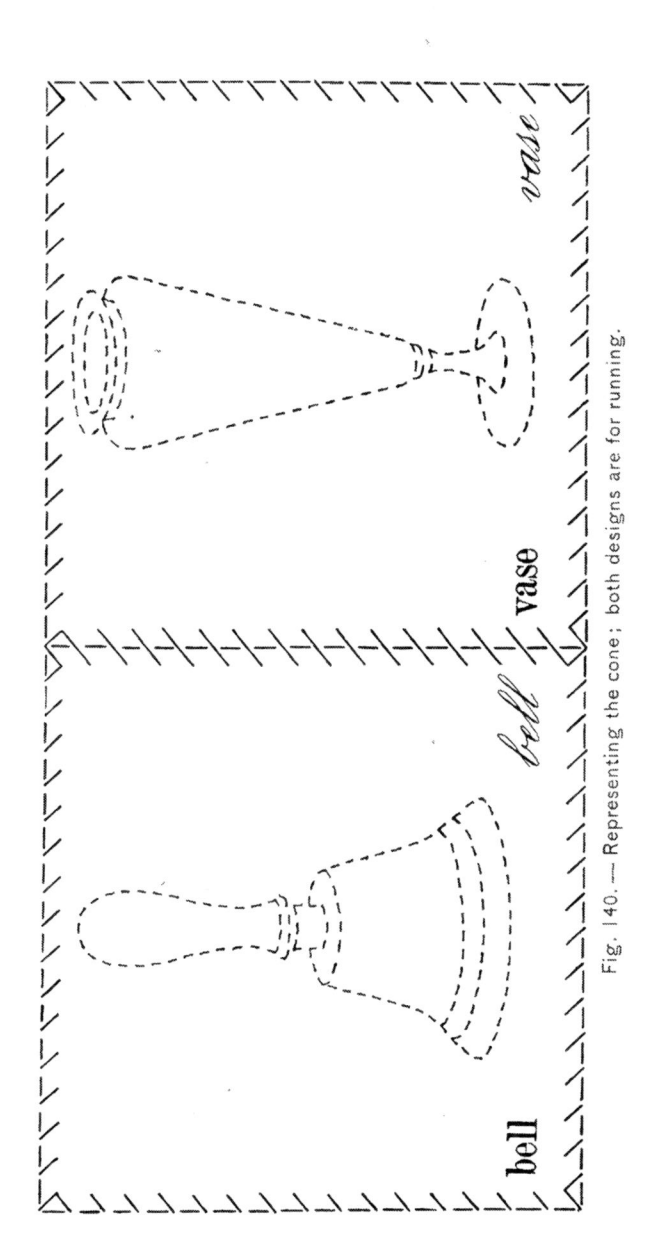

Fig. 140. — Representing the cone; both designs are for running.

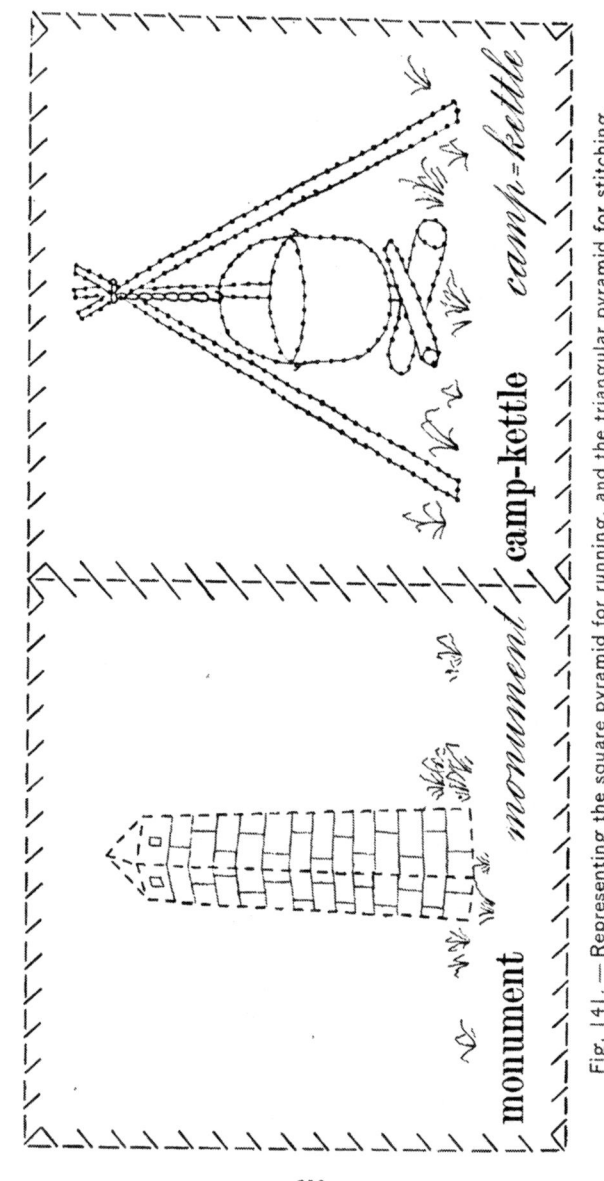

Fig. 141. — Representing the square pyramid for running, and the triangular pyramid for stitching.

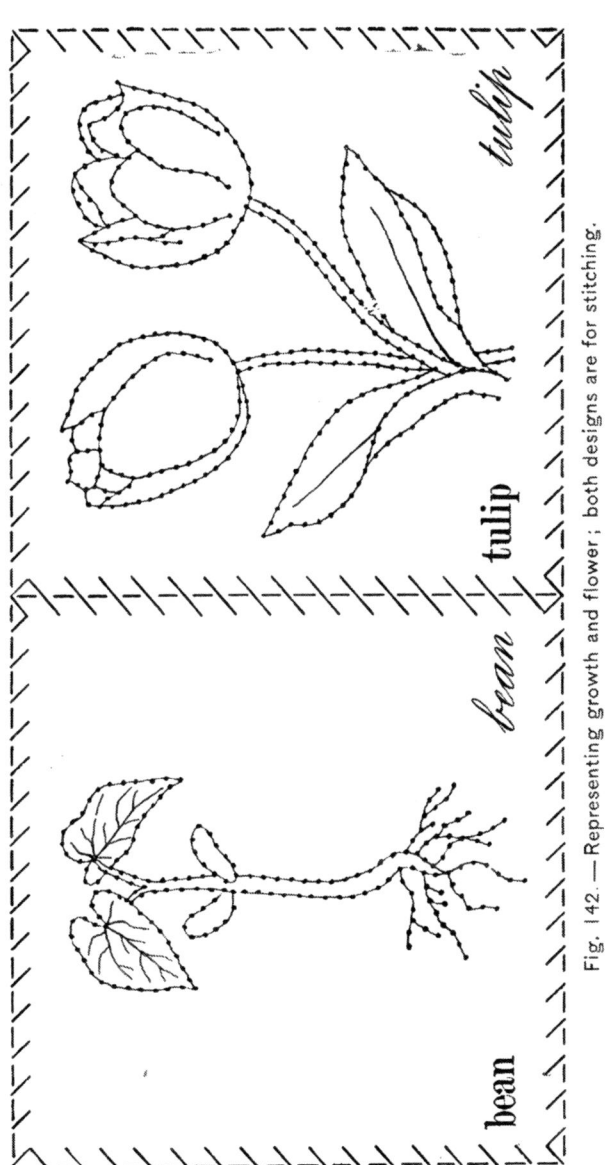

Fig. 142.—Representing growth and flower; both designs are for stitching.

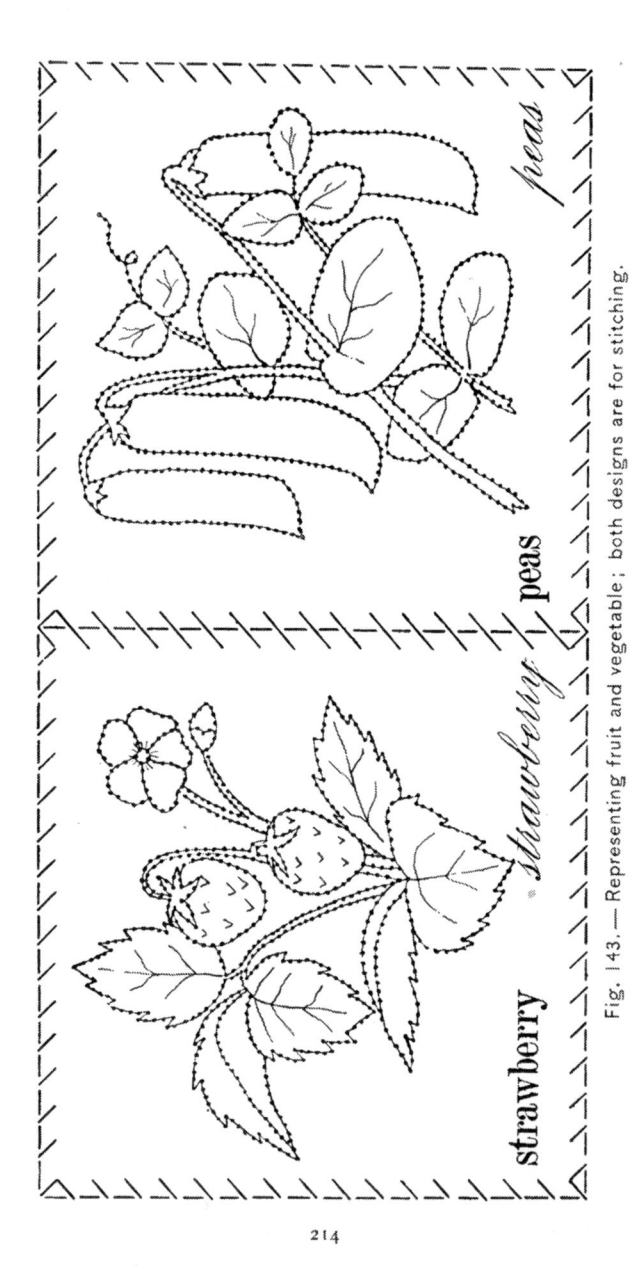

Fig. 143.—Representing fruit and vegetable; both designs are for stitching.

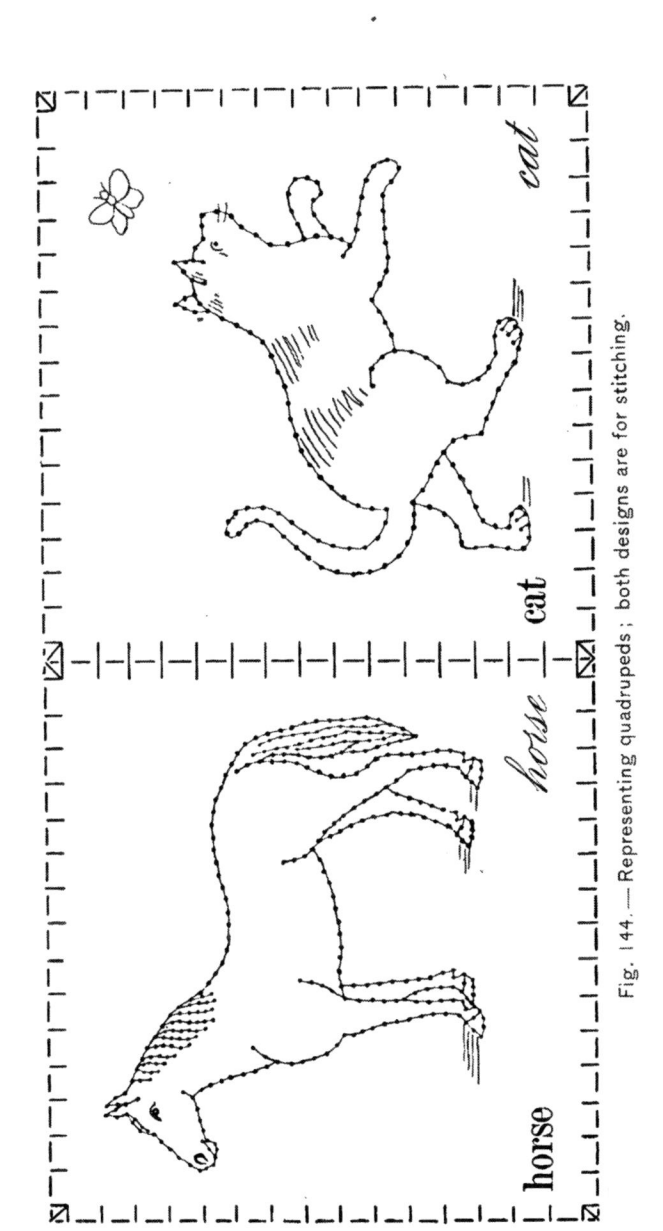

Fig. 144.—Representing quadrupeds; both designs are for stitching.

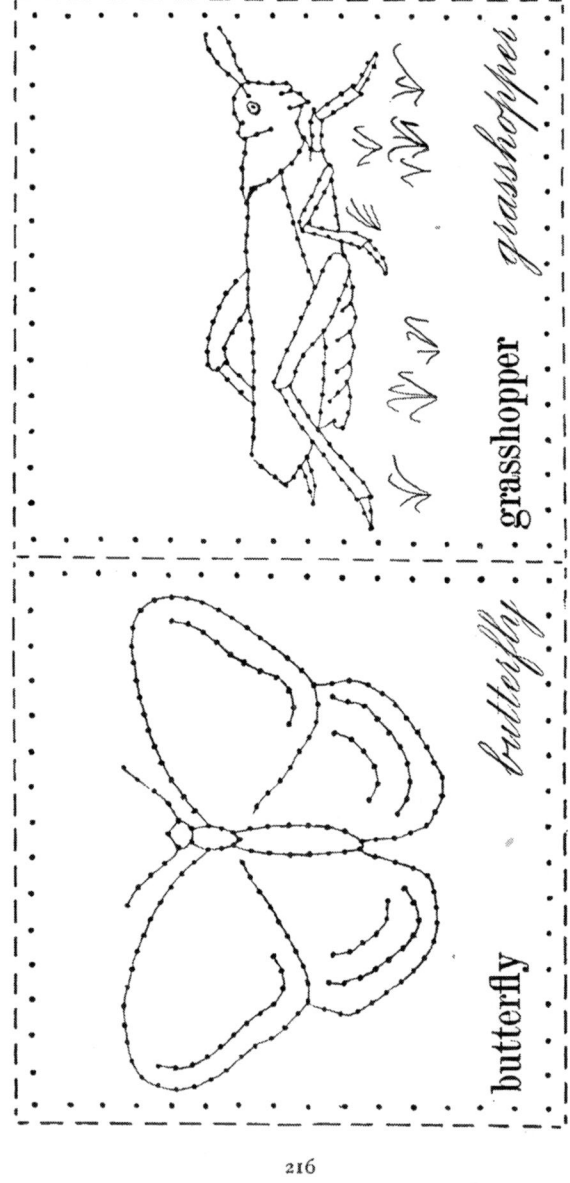

Fig. 145. — Representing insects; both designs are for stitching.

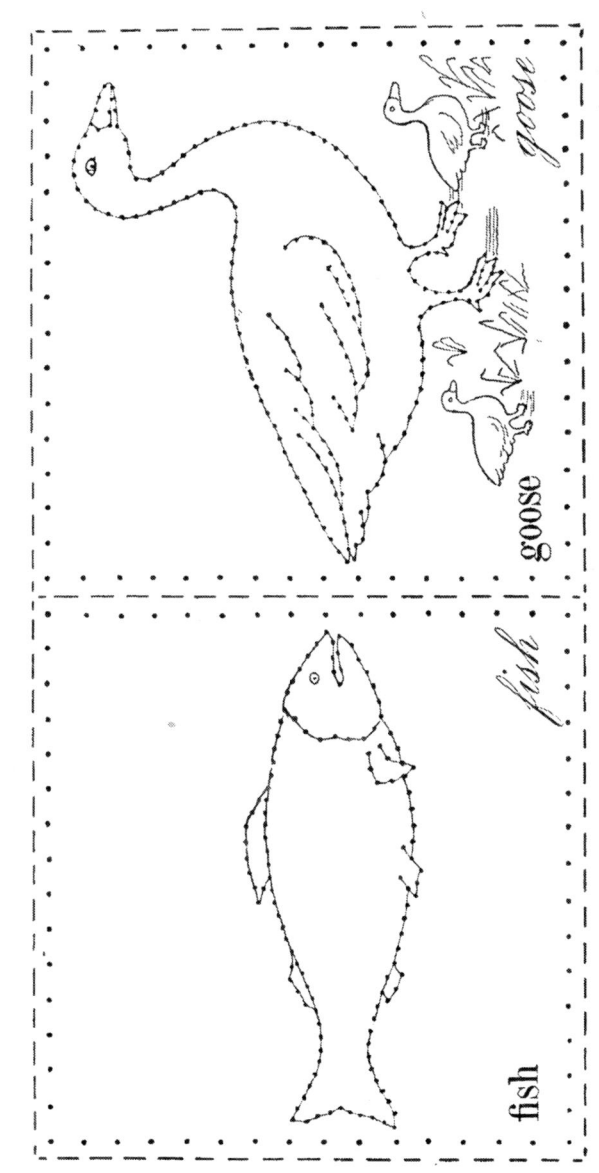

Fig. 146.— Representing an animal of the water, and an animal of water and land; both designs are for stitching.

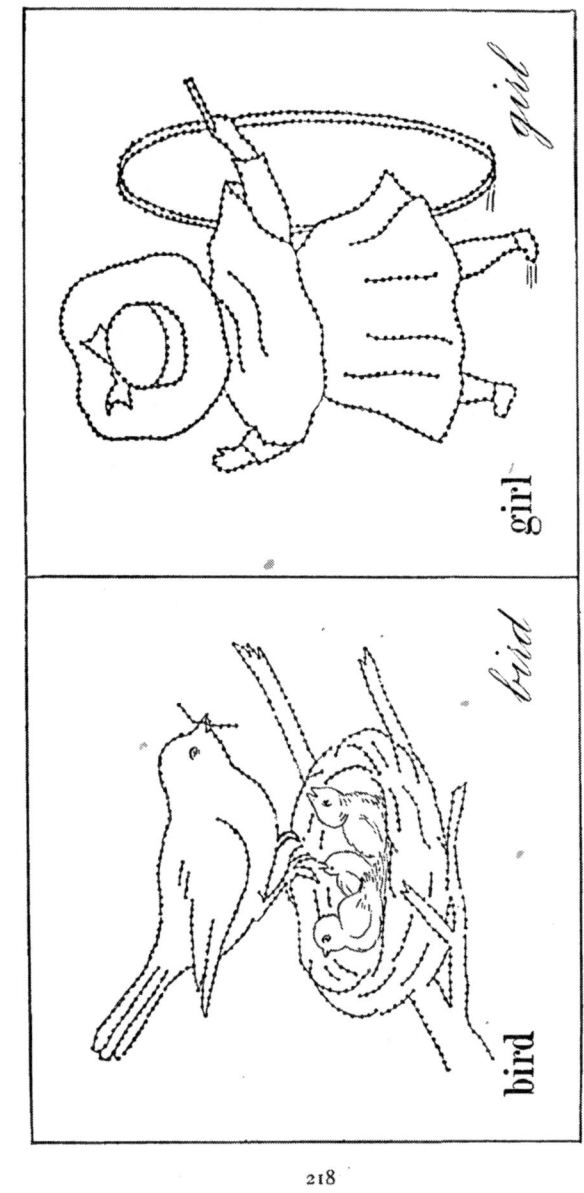

Fig. 148. — Representing a biped and a human being; both designs are for stitching.

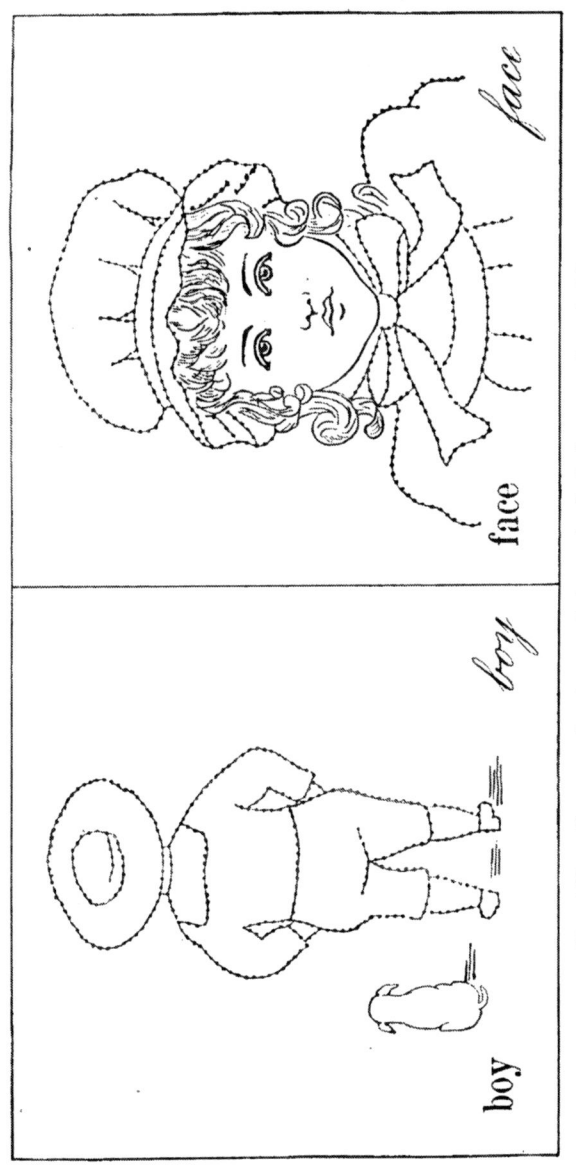

Fig. 149. — Representing human beings; both designs are for stitching.

COURSE OF SEWING FOR INDUSTRIAL SCHOOLS.

In a large school it is necessary to have a test class, in which the pupils are examined as to their ability and proficiency.

PREPARATORY DEPARTMENT.

("Educational Sewing Squares" in use.)

Overcasting of the squares and running of the designs, followed by the same stitches on basted patchwork.

Stitching of the designs, and the stamped, overhanding stitch on the cloth; stitching or overhanding of the squares together.

The overhanding together of the covers of a silk needle-book. If silk or some fine material is used, the children make greater efforts, also if the completed article is to be given to them.

The blanket-stitch on the squares, and on pieces of flannel for leaves of the needle-book.

The stamped, hemming stitch on the cloth, and then on cheap handkerchiefs.

Stitching the seams of a small bag made of nice material.

Overcasting the seams of the bag.

Hemming of the bag.

Catch-stitching on canvas, then on the outside seams of the bag, with bright-colored embroidery silk. The bag on completion is given to the pupil.

Darning over card-board.

Doll's clothes.

ADVANCED CLASSES.
(MAIN SCHOOL.)

The more advanced pupils may be divided into four grades in plain sewing, with special classes for button-hole making, millinery, and embroidery work.

FIRST GRADE.
Unbleached cotton undergarments.
Colored flannel skirts, and towels.
Long-sleeved, dark-colored aprons.

SECOND GRADE.
Half-bleached cotton undergarments.
Gray flannel skirts, and handkerchiefs.
Light-colored calico aprons.

THIRD GRADE.
(THE PUPILS DO THEIR BASTING.)
Bleached cotton undergarments trimmed with ruffles.
Plain white flannel skirts, and white tiers.

FOURTH GRADE.
(THE PUPILS DO THE CUTTING.)
Bleached cotton undergarments trimmed.
White flannel skirts feather-stitched, and white aprons.

FIFTH GRADE.
Dressmaking and machine-stitching.
Millinery and embroidery classes.

When a pupil is ready to make button-holes in a garment, she should go into the button-hole class, where she is also taught to sew on buttons, first practising on the stamped buttons. On the completion of garments the pupils should be allowed to buy them for a small sum. Class bags, plainly marked, should be provided, and also individual bags labeled by a tag fastened to the tape.

FACTS FOR OBSERVATION LESSONS.

(TO BE USED IN CONNECTION WITH THE SEWING CABINET.)

COTTON.

The cotton plant grows on plantations in warm countries. Most of the cotton used in the world is raised in the United States, where the two principal varieties are short-staple cotton or cotton having short fibres, and long-staple cotton having long fibres. The short-staple or upland cotton, which is chiefly raised, grows on a plant from two to three feet in height. Long-staple or sea-island cotton grows fifteen to twenty feet high, and is found on the islands near the coast of the Southern States. Sea-island cotton is much more valuable than upland cotton.

The seed is sown in March and April, and early in June the plant begins to bloom. The blossom resembles that of the hollyhock, and changes its color, being a pale straw-color in the morning, pure white at noon, pale pink at night, and a clear pink the next morning. After the flowers fall, the pods or bolls grow rapidly, and when ripe burst open, showing the fleecy cotton ready for picking, which is done by hand or by a machine.

It is separated from the seeds by being run through the cotton-gin, then baled, and shipped to the manufacturers. The bale is opened, and the cotton is put through a beater and picker-machine, which loosens the matted fibres, and separates a portion of the sand and leaves. It is subjected to a second, and sometimes a third process of picking, which forms it into laps, or rolls of cotton similar to cotton batting.

These laps are taken to the carding-machines, where they are carded, and sometimes combed, until the fibres become sufficiently clean and even ; they are then called slivers. The slivers pass to the drawing-machine, where they are drawn even and parallel, and several of them are united into one. Then they are twisted on the roving-frames into rovings, which are wound upon bobbins. They are next spun into yarn, by passing the rovings through the spinning-machines.

When *thread* is to be made, the yarn is doubled and twisted more than for weaving into cloth, as greater strength is required. It is then reeled off into loose hanks for washing, bleaching and dyeing, after which comes the reeling on to bobbins, and the spooling. In spooling, after the machine-tender has set the spool on the spindle and attached the end of the thread from the bobbin, the machine does the rest. It runs the thread on evenly, without overlapping, or leaving a hair's breadth between, and even adjusts its work with the same precision to the widening of the spool with every layer of thread. It runs on exactly two hundred yards, and at the right time and place, cuts the fine slit in the edge of the spool, draws the end of thread tightly into the slit, cuts it off, and drops the finished spool into a tray. The spools are labeled and packed in boxes containing a dozen each.

If the yarn is to be woven into cloth, the warp is prepared on one machine, and the woof on another ; the warp being made stronger than the woof, as a greater strain comes on it. Then they are woven on the loom, great care being taken that every thread is kept in its proper position. In weaving, the warp threads are first passed from the warp beam at the back of the loom, to the cloth beam in front, on which the cloth is to be wound. Plain weaving is done by passing the woof, in a shuttle, alternately over and under each thread of the warp; this may be readily discerned by unravelling a piece of cotton cloth. Twilled cloth is woven by varying the number of threads passed over or taken up by the woof. In piled cloth, like velvet, other threads are woven in with the woof, making loops, which are afterwards cut and sheared evenly. Mixed cloth is woven with the warp of one color and the woof of another. In striped cloth the warp is of two or more different colors; and in checked cloth the warp and woof are both of two colors, one set of stripes crossing another.

White cloth is bleached after weaving. When calico is made, the cloth is singed, then bleached, and the coloring applied by a printing machine.

WOOL.

Wool is obtained chiefly from the sheep, also from the alpaca, angora, and cashmere goat. It is brought mainly from Australia, South Africa, and South America, but the highest grade is obtained from the merinoes of Saxony and Silesia in Germany.

Wool consists of wavy fibres varying from six to twelve inches in length, and differing in grade. Each fibre is covered with little sawlike teeth or scales overlying each other, and sticking out wherever a bend occurs. The points of the scales are exceedingly small, but when spun, fit into each other and keep the thread from untwisting.

After the wool has been sheared from the sheep, which is done yearly, it is separated according to fineness and length of fibre into sorts, by experienced men called sorters. Then, as it is full of grease and dirt, it is scoured by being immersed in successive vats of hot, alkaline lye, varying in strength, until most of the impurities are removed. After scouring, the wool is dried, and it is then ready for further processes. At this point the question must be decided whether the fabric to be manufactured is to be a woollen or a worsted.

Formerly, woollen goods were made from short-fibred wool with high felting properties, while worsted goods were made from long-fibred wool with poor felting properties, but now, from many kinds of wool both woollens and worsteds can be made, the distinction between them being caused by the different processes to which the wool is subjected.

We will first describe the method of manufacturing *woollens*. After the wool is scoured, it is passed through a willowing-machine in order to remove any dirt or dust that may still adhere to it, and also to break up the matted pieces. Then it is carded, by which the wool is thoroughly cleaned from sticks and lumps, and the fibres are torn apart and then interlaced with each other, coming out in the form of a loose rope called sliver, in which the separate fibres stand in an infinite variety of positions with reference to each other. If the fabric is to be wool-dyed, the next process is the dyeing, after which it is drawn down by drawing, roving and spinning frames into a woollen yarn.

If greater strength is required, two or more strands are twisted together, making a woollen thread ready for the loom. If the fabric is to be yarn-dyed, the dyeing process occurs at this stage. The yarn is now woven into cloth. It is fulled by being soaked in hot, soapy water, and subjected to heavy pressure, thus causing the fibres to felt together, and the cloth to shrink in width. The fabric is now compact and firm, and is ready for the finishing processes. The fibres are loosened and raised to form a nap, by passing the surface of the cloth over the sharp little hooks of the teasel, which are set in rollers. Teasels are the flower heads of a variety of thistle. Then the cloth is sheared to give a uniform surface, and it is passed between steam rollers in order to receive the smooth, glossy finish that renders it attractive.

The processes used in making a *worsted* fabric are different from those just described in several respects. The object is to make a yarn in which the fibres shall be drawn out parallel to each other, and then twisted to the required degree.

The wool is put through various machines to straighten out the fibres, and to take out those that are too short for use. Long wools are put through preparers; shorter wools are passed through carding-machines, both of which bring the wool into a loose sliver, which, after being back-washed and slightly oiled, is passed through a combing-machine, where the short fibres, called noils, are combed out, and there is formed a firm, smooth, clean rope made up of long, parallel fibres loosely adhering to each other.

This rope is wound into balls or wool tops, about one foot in diameter. Then follow the processes of drawing, roving, spinning and twisting, care being taken to preserve the substantial parallel relation of the fibres to each other, until a smooth, level yarn is formed ready for weaving into cloth.

After the cloth is woven it is dyed, if that has not been done in the yarn, and it is then ready for the finishing, which differs slightly from the method pursued in making woollens. The cloth is not teazled, and is only slightly fulled, sometimes not at all. It is singed by being passed at a high rate of speed over a hot roller ; is steamed, stretched, and pressed between rollers, and is then put up in proper shape for sale.

LINEN.

Linen thread and cloth are made from the fibres of the flax plant. The coverings in which the Egyptian mummies have been found enveloped, prove that flax has been used from the remotest times in the manufacture of linen cloth. In the British Museum pieces of linen four thousand years old may be seen. The best qualities of flax come from France and The Netherlands.

The plant grows to a height of two or three feet, and bears delicate blue flowers. The stalks of the plant are hollow, and consist of a woody portion called the boon, and a fibrous portion from which the thread is made. The seeds furnish linseed-oil, used for mixing paints. If a fine fibre is desired, the stalks are pulled up by the roots, when the leaves begin to fall off and the bottom of the stalks become yellow. By waiting until the seeds are ripe, a coarser fibre and seeds for oil are obtained.

After being dried in the sun, the seeds are removed, and the stalks soaked or retted in water to loosen the fibres from the boon. The fibres are dried and run through rollers, which break the boon. Then they are combed out or disentangled, and the wood removed by the scutching-machine. The flax, now ready for the mill, is put through the hackling-machine, where the short fibres are separated from the long. The long fibres are called line and go through the spread-board, while the short fibres, called tow, pass through the carding-machine; both varieties entering cans called sliver-cans. The sliver then passes through a number of drawing-frames, and after being doubled and drawn out, it goes to the roving-frame, where it is again drawn out, then twisted and wound on to bobbins. The rovings are spun on the spinning-frames and reduced to yarn, which is either woven into cloth or twisted into thread. The linen is bleached for white goods, or dyed for colored.

During all the operations the fibres must be kept wet with warm water, to render them pliable.

Various kinds of heavy cloth, such as canvas, coarse toweling, tent-cloth and bagging, are made from *hemp*, which is prepared and wove similar to flax.

SILK.

There is no more interesting subject than the source and manufacture of silk. The manufacture of silk doubtless originated in China. Although some silkworms are raised in this country, the greater part of the raw silk is imported from China and Europe.

The silkworm moth lays the eggs from which the silkworms are hatched, and they in turn become moths. The moth is about an inch long, having white wings marked with broad pale-brown bars. One moth lays from three hundred to seven hundred eggs, so small that it takes three or four hundred eggs to cover a space as large as a silver dollar. In a warm, dry temperature the eggs will hatch in a few days. The young silkworm or caterpillar is dark-colored, and not more than a quarter of an inch in length. When full grown the worm is about three inches long; the body is made up of twelve joints, and it has sixteen legs. It reaches maturity in about a month, and during this time feeds upon the leaves of the mulberry tree, requiring constant feeding; it also changes its skin four times. When about to spin its cocoon on some convenient branch or roll of paper, it ceases to eat.

The silk is produced from two small bags filled with a liquid gum. From each bag comes a slender tube, which unites into one tube near the mouth, through which the gum is drawn and spun into silk; thus each fibre of silk, when examined under a microscope, is seen to consist of two strands, one from each bag. The silkworm first makes an outer covering of coarse fibres called floss-silk, then, bending itself like a horseshoe, and moving its head from one point to another, it entirely surrounds the body with silk, not spun regularly around the cocoon, but back and forth, so that sometimes yards may be unwound without turning over the cocoon. The inner silk is the finest. The cocoon is completed in a few days, and is about the size of a pigeon's egg. If left undisturbed, in two or three weeks the moth will eat its way through the cocoon, and in so doing break and injure the silk; to prevent this, it is stifled or killed by heat.

Each cocoon contains about one-fourth of a mile of thread, as fine as a cobweb, and it takes three thousand cocoons to make a pound of silk. The cocoons are first sorted, and the outside threads removed. They are next placed in tepid water, where they are stirred until the ends of four or five threads are found and brought together into a single thread, which is wound on to a reel. Then it goes to the spinning-frames, where it is doubled and twisted into the various sizes required for sewing-silk or for weaving.

The silk after being cleaned (all the knots or obstructions removed) and dried, is ready to be colored and woven into fabric on the loom. Silk is the strongest of all fibres used for weaving.

The reeling or spinning of the silk is very difficult, as the cocoons differ in color, quality and length. The silk on the outside of the cocoon, and that near the chrysalis is inferior and broken; so this, with that from cocoons which have been injured, is made into what is called spun-silk. Raw silk is made from the perfect cocoons.

SCISSORS AND SHEARS.

Scissors and shears are made in various sizes and styles; strictly speaking, every pair over six inches in length should be called shears. Those made from steel are manufactured almost entirely in Germany; in this country malleable iron with steel for the inside edges is used. Nearly all the work is done by hand, but the process of making depends somewhat upon the size. Each pair passes through the hands of fifty or sixty workmen before completion.

The iron is first melted at the foundry and run into moulds of the different shapes desired. The steel is run into thin sheets, which are cut into strips, and these are punched, and riveted to the iron by one blow of a hammer. These pieces are then dipped in water and again in powdered borax, to cleanse the surfaces of the iron and steel, which would not unite without this process. After being heated red hot in a furnace, the two metals are welded together, and shaped by a die or stamp.

A large pair of shears is used to trim the steel, that protrudes over the blades; after which the blades pass through the hands of a number of workmen, each doing his part towards shaping the shears. They are hardened by being plunged while red hot into a tank of cold water, which renders them very brittle. To remedy the brittleness they are put on a plate and again heated, until the workman knows by the color that they are properly tempered or toughened.

After various processes, in one of which the hole for the screw is drilled, a temporary screw is put in, and the points and handles adjusted. This screw is taken out and the blades are numbered, in order that they may be kept in pairs. They are ground on a round stone, making a slight hollow on the surface of the blades; this forms an edge to cut on. A small elevation is also made close behind the screw, which causes the blades to cant more and more towards each other as they are closed. Then the handles are japanned or nickel-plated, and the blades are polished on emery wheels. After this they are taken to a stamping-machine, where the maker's name is put on them. Then the edges of the blades are sharpened on fine emery wheels, the screw is put in, and the blades adjusted.

Lastly they are carefully inspected, packed in boxes, and are ready for market.

NEEDLES.

Needles have been used by the women of every country, in every age. Bronze needles have been found in Egyptian tombs, and we have mention of them in the early history of the Greeks and Romans.

The common sewing needle is made from steel wire, and is manufactured almost exclusively in England. Although simple in form, a needle passes through the hands of a hundred workmen before completion. The wire is cut from coils into pieces or blanks of twice the required length of the needle. After being straightened, the blanks are ground to a point at both ends, and flattened in the middle; on this flattened surface the groove for the thread is made, also two small indentations to mark the places for the eyes, which are drilled by machinery. The lengths are now separated, and are hardened by being heated and dipped in oil; then they are tempered by again slowly heating and cooling. After being scoured, rounded and polished, they are sorted, and folded in papers, which, when labelled, are put up in packages.

Machine needles are manufactured in this country by machines invented for the purpose. The work is similar to that done on the common needle, machines being substituted for part of the hand labor.

PINS.

Pins similar to those now in use were not known in ancient times, when thorns, and bone, wooden, gold or silver skewers were used to fasten the clothing. In the sixteenth century, when first manufactured, they were so expensive that only the rich could afford to buy them; when first made in the United States, a paper of pins cost one dollar.

Pins are now manufactured by machines and are made in many sizes. The wire, after being reduced to the proper size and condition, is run through a machine, which cuts it into the required length, forms the head, and also sharpens the point and tempers it. The pins are next cleaned, and the imperfect ones thrown out by machinery. The third machine rolls them until they are bright and smooth. Another machine sticks them into the paper, and, after being inspected under a magnifying glass, they are ready for market. A machine has been invented which does the entire work. Black pins are prepared by japanning the common pins.

THIMBLES.

Thimbles have been in use only about two hundred years. They are made of metal, celluloid, or aluminum, with either an open or closed top. The indentations on the surface are made to hold the head of the needle firmly.

In manufacturing metal thimbles, a thin disk or blank, about the size of a silver half-dollar, is first cut from sheet metal, and is then drawn into a cap. This cap is heated and tapered, and the edges rolled; the top and then the sides are indented, and it is completed by being polished and plated.

BUTTONS.

Buttons are made from many materials, and in many sizes and shapes. The cheapest are made of porcelain, which is pressed into moulds and baked.

Vegetable ivory buttons are made from the seeds of the ivory plant. The plant grows on the Isthmus of Panama, and resembles a palm. The fruit is round, from eight to twelve inches in diameter, and weighs about twenty-five pounds. It is composed of six or seven portions, each portion containing from six to nine seeds. These seeds, when ripe, are pure white, free from veins or any dots, and are about two inches in diameter. The substance is so hard that it can be readily turned in the lathe.

The seeds or nuts are sawed into slabs, from which the buttons are turned. The next operation is that of drilling the holes; some buttons are drilled with four holes, others with two holes, while others are not drilled, but have what is called a self-shank.

After being dyed or colored they are finished by polishing and mottling. Horn and bone buttons are made in a similar manner.

Cloth-covered button. — In the manufacture of cloth-covered buttons, two round pieces of cloth, one for the covering and one for the shank, two collets of tin and a thick paper filling are used. The tuft of strong linen is placed in the under collet, and a die or stamp comes down, and presses the tuft through the collet, making the flexible shank by which the button is sewed on. The cloth covering is then placed on the upper collet or shell, and pressed up into a die. Just before the die holding the upper part of the button is pressed into the one holding the under part, the paper filling is put in. As the dies come together they turn the edge of the shell over the collet, and the different parts are thus held strongly together.

Flat metal button. — The four-holed metal button is manufactured from collets or disks cut from sheet metal. The under collet of the button is cut from tin, the upper collet from brass. Then the collets are shaped and the four holes punched by a machine. A piece of strawboard of the same form is prepared, and the three pieces are bound together by solidly lapping the edge of the brass or larger collet over the other two.

Hollow gilt button with shank. — This button consists of three pieces of brass, — the front, back and the wire eye. The manufacture is described in the following steps, which may be readily understood if samples are shown.

Front. — 1. Blanking, or cutting out the round disk from the sheet. 2. Stamping, or raising the figure. 3. Annealing, or softening after the stamping. 4. Pickling, or removing the oxide produced by the annealing. 5. Drawing or shaping the front. 6. Annealing. 7. Pickling. 8. Cleaning, or removing by acids the scales produced upon the surface during the manufacture of the metal. 9. Lacquering the inside. 10. Drying the lacquer, which has been applied to the inside of the front, in order that in the process of fire-gilding no gold may be wasted by attaching itself to the inside. 11. Cleaning, or preparing for the gold. 12. Gilding, showing the result after the gold has been applied. The application of this gold is by what is known as the "fire gilding process," in which the gold is first dissolved in mercury, and applied to the surface of the metal. After this the mercury is volatilized in an oven and passes up the chimney from the oven, leaving the gold in chemical contact with the surface of the metal. 13. Scratching, or brightening by rubbing with a bunch of fine wire. 14. Coloring, or bringing out the color of the gold. 15. Burnishing, or brightening the surface of the letters with a burnishing-stone.

Back. — 1. Cutting and bending the wire for the eye. 2. Blanking, or cutting out the round disk from the sheet. 3. Heading, or attaching the eye to the back. 4. Charging, or placing of the soldering paste about the wire. 5. Soldering. 6. Cleaning, by immersion in acids. 7. Stamping into shape, including the embossing of the letters. 8. Silvering. 9. Burnishing.

Uniting. — 1. Closing, or uniting of the front and the back, both of which have been separately finished.

2. Edging, or burnishing of the extreme edge. 3. Bottoming, or burnishing of the edge and the back. 4. Beveling, or burnishing of the edge and the front side. 5. Finished button.

HOOKS AND EYES.

Hooks and eyes are manufactured from wire by machinery. Two hundred hooks and the same number of eyes, each being made by its own machine, can be manufactured in a minute. The wire, on being unwound from a reel, is cut into the required length, and drawn into the machine, where it is bent into shape and comes out completed. They are silvered or blackened with japan varnish.

The machines run automatically, all that the machine tender has to do is to see that they are supplied with wire. The hooks and eyes have to be sewed and stuck on to cardboard by hand.

EMERY.

Emery is a variety of corundum, and is ranked among the hardest of minerals. It derives its name from Cape Emeri on the island of Naxos, Grecian Archipelago, where the best variety is obtained. It is also found in a number of places in the United States.

It is used for polishing metals. The stone is crushed and sifted into powder of different fineness.

WAX.

Bees-wax is an animal secretion, formed by the bees, and constitutes the material of which the cells of the honey-comb are composed. After the honey is removed, the wax is dirty, tough and yellow. To make it pure and white, the wax is melted and stirred in boiling water ; when cooled the pure wax rises to the top. It is again melted, and then bleached in the open air, until it becomes white. It is finally melted, strained through sieves and cast in molds.

SCHOOL-CABINET.

A very interesting school-cabinet can be made by procuring the following named articles,[1] and pictures of the different machines used in their manufacture. They may be put into mounting-boxes or fastened on to cards, and thus easily shown the pupils.

Cotton. — 1. Cotton seeds. 2. Roots and stalks. 3. Leaves and blossoms. 4. Pods or bolls. 5. Sample from cotton-gin. 6. Sample from combined beating and scutching-machine, called laps. 7. Sample from carding or combing-machine, called sliver. 8. Sample from drawing-machine, still called sliver. 9. Samples from the different roving-machines, called rovings. 10. Sample from ring-frame, called warp. 11. Sample from mule-frame, called filling or woof. 12. Samples of thread. 13. Sample of unbleached cloth from the loom. 14. Sample of bleached cloth. 15. Samples of the various kinds of cotton cloth.

Wool. — 1. Samples of wool on the hide of both the sheep and the goat. 2. Sample of wool sheared from the sheep. 3. Sample after being scoured and dried. 4. Sample from the willowing-machine. 5. Sample from the carding-machine. 6. Sample from the drawing-machine. 7. Samples from the roving-machines. 8. Samples from the spinning-frames. 9. Samples of yarn. 10. Sample of woollen cloth from the loom. 11. Sample after

---

[1] The author has five hundred specimens, besides illustrations.

being fulled. 12. Sample after being teaseled and sheared. 13. Teasels. 14. Sample after being finished. 15. Sample of worsted cloth from the loom. 16. Sample after being scoured and dried. 17. Sample after being dyed and rough dried. 18. Sample after being finished. 19. Samples of camel's hair in the different processes. 20. Samples of the various kinds of woollen and worsted goods.

Linen. — 1. Flax-seeds. 2. Roots and stalks. 3. Leaves and blossoms. 4. Sample after being retted and dried. 5. Sample after being broken to crack the wood or boon. 6. Sample after being scutched and freed from the boon, called rough flax. 7. Sample from hackling-machine, called line. 8. Sample from hackling-machine, called tow. 9. Sample from spread-board, called sliver. 10. Sample from carding-machine. 11. Sample from drawing-machine. 12. Samples from roving-frames. 13. Samples from spinning-frames. 14. Samples of thread. 15. Sample of unbleached cloth from the loom. 16. Sample of bleached cloth. 17. Samples of the various kinds of linen cloth.

Silk. — 1. Mulberry leaves. 2. Eggs. 3. Silkworms. 4. Cocoons. 5. Cocoon cut lengthwise into halves showing chrysalis. 6. Moth leaving cocoon. 7. Moth. 8. Silk spun from cocoon. 9. Samples from the reeling-machines. 10. Samples from the spinning-frames. 11. Samples of thread. 12. Sample from the loom. 13. Samples of the various kinds of silk fabrics.

Scissors. — 1. Iron ore and nickel. 2. Blades moulded from iron. 3. Steel riveted to the blades. 4. Steel and iron welded together. 5. Blades trimmed. 6. Blades tempered. 7. Points and handles adjusted. 8. Blades numbered and ground. 9. Nickel-plated or handles japanned. 10. Finished scissors.

Needles. — 1. Steel wire or blank. 2. Ends sharpened. 3. Groove made. 4. Eyes punched. 5. Lengths separated. 6. Finished needle.

Sewing-machine needles. — 1. Blank. 2. Ends pointed. 3. Swaged or compressed. 4. Clipped. 5. Stamped (name and size). 6. Pointed. 7. Grooved. 8. Eye punched. 9. Hardened. 10. Polished. 11. Finished.

Pins. — 1. Brass wire. 2. Head formed. 3. Ends sharpened. 4. Finished pins after whitening or japanning.

Thimbles. — 1. Blank. 2. Cap. 3. Cap tapered. 4. Edge trimmed. 5. Flange rolled. 6. Flange finished and milled. 7. Top indented. 8. Sides indented. 9. Plated thimble. 10. Various kinds of thimbles.

Buttons. — *Vegetable Ivory button.* — 1. Nut or seed. 2. Sawed into slabs. 3. Button turned from the slab, and slab as it remains. 4. Holes drilled. 5. Finished button.

Metal button. — 1. Upper collet of brass. 2. Under collet of tin. 3. Straw-board filling. 4. Finished button.

Cloth-covered button. — 1. Shell, or upper collet. 2. Under collet. 3. Paper filling. 4. Round piece of linen for tuft. 5. Round piece of woollen cloth for covering. 6. Finished button.

Hollow gilt button with shank. — 1. Blanking. 2. Stamping. 3. Annealing. 4. Pickling off. 5. Drawing. 6. Annealing. 7. Pickling off. 8. Cleaning. 9. Lacquering. 10. Drying off. 11. Cleaning. 12. Gilding. 13. Scratching. 14. Coloring. 15. Burnishing. 16. Wire for eye. 17. Eye bent. 18. Blanking for back. 19. Heading. 20. Charging. 21. Soldering. 22. Cleaning. 23. Stamping. 24. Silvering. 25. Burnishing. 26. Closing. 27. Edging. 28. Bottoming. 29. Beveling. 30. Finished button.

Hooks and Eyes. — *Hooks.* — 1. Wire. 2. Wire bent for loop. 3. Small circles formed. 4. Loop bent over. 5. Loop flattened. 6. Hook silvered or japanned.

Eyes. — 1. Wire. 2. Wire bent for loop. 3. Small circles formed. 4. Eye silvered or japanned.

Emery. — 1. Emery-stone. 2. Powder. 3. Emery-bag.

Wax. — 1. Bee. 2. Honey-comb. 3. Yellow and white wax.

INDEX TO TEACHER'S EDITION.

Alphabets, 126, 127, 128.
Articles needed, 1.
A-shopping expedition, 177.
Basting, 21, 167.
Bias piecing, 109.
Bindings, 46.
   Stitching and hemming, 46.
   Setting in, 49.
   Overhanding, 51.
Blackboard, 181.
Blanket-stitch, 122.
Blind-stitch, 77.
Boys' sewing, 185.
Button-holes, 53, 163, 179.
Buttons, 61, 234, 241.
Canvas-work, 18, 169.
Catch-stitch, 117.
Chain-stitch, 120.
Cloth, 8.
Collection of work, 186.
Compositions, 184.
Corners mitred, 111.
Cotton, 222, 239.
Course of sewing, 172.
Creasing, 19, 167.
Cutting, 10, 129, 169.
   Two-breadth apron, 133.
   Child's bib, 134.
   Pockets, 135.
   Child's drawers, 137.
   Night-dress yoke, 139.

Child's sack tier, 142.
Gored skirt, 148.
Drawers, 149.
Child's waist, 153.
Hints for a plain basque, 156.
Doll's patterns, 159.
Dark days, 177.
DARNING —
   Cloth darning, 93, 169.
      Straightway-darn, 93.
      Bias-darn, 95.
      Corner-darn, 96.
      Darning with a piece underneath, 97.
      Fine drawing on heavy woollen material, 98.
   Stockinet darning, 85.
      Practice in weaving, 85.
      Stockinet darning, 86.
      Grafting, 89.
      Swiss-darning, 90.
      Stocking-web stitch, 90.
Demonstration lessons, 163.
Directions for sewing, 2.
Drafting, 132, 169.
Drawing lessons, 182.
Drills, 14, 163.
Dropping articles, 178.
Edgings, 78.
   Lace, 78.
   Hamburg, 80.

Educational Sewing Squares for Primary Work, 199.
Embroidery knots, 124.
Emery, 237, 242.
Examinations, 185.
Exhibitions, 184.
Eyelet-holes, 63.
Facings, 52.
Fancy-work, 178.
Feather-stitch, 119, 169.
Felling, 75.
Fractions of a yard, 13.
French hem on damask, 77.
French seam, 76.
Gathering, 36, 168.
    Double gathering, 40.
    Placing or stroking of gathers, 38.
Grafting, 89.
Gussets, 66.
Gusset and facing combined, 69.
Half-backstitching, 25.
Hemming, 25, 167.
Hem-stitch, 115.
Herringbone-stitch, 117.
Honey-combing, 44.
Hooks and eyes, 64, 237, 242.
How to keep the pupils busy, 167.
Industrial schools, course of sewing for, 220.
Kensington outline-stitch, 121.
Kindergarten sewing, 187.
Knots, 7.
Linen, 227, 240.
Loops, 65.
Loops of tape, 113.
Marking, 125, 169.
Measure, 13.
Mitring the corner of a hem, 112.

Mitring two strips of cloth, 111.
Mounting models, 185.
Needles, 4, 232, 241.
Numbers of needles and thread, 8.
Overcasting, 31, 168.
Overhanding, 33.
Patching, 100, 169.
    Hemming, 100.
    Overhanding, 103.
    Catch-stitching, 105.
Pins, 233, 241.
Piping, 110.
Placket, 70.
Plaiting, 73, 168.
Primary sewing, 199.
Putting away the work, 2.
Ruffles, 80.
Running, 28, 168.
Running and a backstitch, 30.
Sampler, 179.
Scalloped edge, 43.
Scissors, 10, 178, 230, 240.
Shirring, 42.
Silk, 228, 240.
Simultaneous teaching, 163.
Sinistrous pupils, 178.
Slip-stitch, 77.
Smocking, 44.
Stitching, 23.
Stocking-web stitch, 90.
Thimbles, 234, 241.
Thread, 5, 167.
Threading the needle, 6.
Trial-piece, 166.
Tucking, 71.
Wax, 238, 242.
Whipping, 82, 168.
Wool, 224, 239.